PEAKBAGGING
MONTANA

A GUIDE TO MONTANA'S MAJOR PEAKS

Text, maps, photos by Cedron Jones

Cover and text design by DD Dowden

FRONT COVER: Sundance Pass, Beartooth Mtns. (Cedron Jones photo);
Trapper Peak (Christopher Cauble photo)
TITLE PAGE PHOTO: Torrey Lake from Tweedy Mtn., East Pioneers (Cedron Jones photo)

RIVERBEND PUBLISHING
P.O. Box 5833
Helena, MT 59604
www.riverbendpublishing.com

Disclaimer
The author and publisher do not assume and hereby disclaim any responsibility or liability for damages, losses, or injuries that might occur to those using the information in this book. Hiking, scrambling, and climbing all have potential hazards involving risk of injury or death. Although information in this book is intended to assist in locating and following peakbagging routes, it is neither represented nor guaranteed to be accurate or complete. Mountain conditions change from day to day and season to season, rendering any information subject to change without warning. Those who use this information, and those who venture onto mountainous terrain, do so at their own risk.

Additionally, some of the peaks or portions of routes described in this book are on private land. Neither the author nor the publisher encourage trespassing on private land and hereby disclaim any responsibility or liability for anyone doing so. It is the individual's responsibility to secure permission to travel on private land.

Contents

Peaks above Miner Lake Basin, West Big Hole.

Dedication

I love this gorgeous and grand thing called Earth.
In John Denver's words, it "fills up my senses."
My hope is this book will enable a few folks to experience more of its grandeur
and be motivated to help it gain the full measure of love and respect it deserves.

Acknowledgments

I am grateful to three groups of folks for helping make this book possible: first and foremost, to my wife Sara and friends Bill Bucher, Gretchen Rupp and Mark Shapley, who often accompanied me on explorations—both 'winners' and 'losers'—and came back for more even after a real 'loser' of a trip.

Secondly, I'm grateful to the community of peakbaggers, data nerds and prominence geeks who expanded my knowledge and provided many of the resources to not only conceive of and write this book, but, more importantly, to pursue many wonderful peaks I would otherwise have overlooked. I've never met any of them but have exchanged collective emails with Andy Martin, Greg Slayden, Adam Helman, Aaron Maizlish, Eric Noel, John Kirk and Jerry & Betty Brekhus.

Finally, I owe thanks to the folks who helped turn the idea for the book into what you lovingly cradle in your hands right now. Foremost among them is DD Dowden, whose artistry turned my text & maps into a beautiful book. Christian Frazza, Gregg Wheeler, Dan Sullivan, and Bill Bucher reviewed the text. The Natural Resources Information System (NRIS) in the Montana State Library provided the base map used for the locator maps, and Gerry Daumiller at NRIS provided invaluable help with maps and GNIS data.

ALL ROYALTIES FROM SALES OF THIS BOOK ARE SHARED BETWEEN THE
MONTANA WILDERNESS ASSOCIATION,
WILDERNESS WATCH, AND
THE CINNABAR FOUNDATION

Introduction

I'm not sure when I became a peakbagger. I hiked some as a Boy Scout and some more during college, when I worked a few summers in national parks washing dishes and hauling trash. It may have been when I moved to Boston to attend graduate school and bought an Appalachian Mountain Club (AMC) White Mountain Guide. In the Introduction there is a section on "The Four Thousand Footer Club"—complete with a list of peaks and a blank column labeled "Date Climbed." The earliest date I have penciled in is "9/68"; so perhaps that's when I got the bug. But I suspect that bagging a peak back then was just incidental to going out for a hike.

By the time I turned 40, I was going on extended trips around western Montana with the specific goal of climbing mountains, and I had started a diary to record my climbs. Though I occasionally sought out a peak, like Granite Peak in the Beartooth Mountains or Borah Peak in Idaho, because of its inclusion on a list (e.g., state highpoints), those trips were essentially explorations. I would buy a National Forest Visitors Map for the area I wanted to explore, find a peak that sounded interesting or appeared to be high, figure out how to get there and climb it, and while on top pick out and identify my next objective.

That carefree and spontaneous approach began to transform shortly after moving to Helena, Montana, in 1985. Suddenly, through my work, I had access to a complete set of topographic maps for the state. By carefully perusing those maps, I was able to create lists of peaks—Montana's hundred highest, the highpoint of every mountain range, every peak in the state!—and then go try to bag them.

I have now climbed more than 1200 Montana peaks, including all 340 of Montana's 10,000 footers (p400 standard). I have climbed all of the mountain range highpoints in this book except for four on private land. I have not climbed all of the county highpoints—some are on private land and some aren't really peaks (as defined in the book).

I say I have "climbed" these peaks, but this book is not about technical climbing. I am primarily a hiker, and this book is for hikers, scramblers, and "peakbaggers."

Rocky Mountain (on the right), Sawtooth Range.

What is peakbagging?

Peakbagging is essentially climbing mountains, but with a few critical differences—at least as used in this guide.

The first is the nature of the motivation. Mountain climbers plan their trips based on the allure of a certain peak—its beauty, its reputation, the quality of its rock or snow or ice. Peakbaggers choose a peak based on its inclusion in one or more lists. Climbing all the peaks on the list is the real goal, more so than attaining any particular summit. This might involve walking around in thick woods or on a gentle prairie hill, trying to find the highest point of some obscure "peak" on your list. It can also require climbing a summit that is surrounded by clearcuts or mines, or plastered with towers and buildings. Aesthetics are still important to peakbaggers, but peakbagging demands open-mindedness, an appreciation for diversity, and a positive attitude. (There *are* list-less peakbaggers who could care less about "highest" this or "biggest" that or any other kind of list.)

The second difference is the approach, figuratively and often literally, to the climb. Mountain climbers are interested in aesthetics, originality, competition, personal growth. Hence they are often more concerned with the route followed than with actually reaching the top. Peakbaggers, in contrast, just want to get to the summit and check it off their list. They generally seek out the easiest or quickest way to the top, though some "official" list-keepers have standards addressing, for example, climbing routes for peaks that have roads to the summit.

What kinds of peak lists are there?

As many as one can imagine: every peak over 11,000 feet; every peak in the Bob Marshall Wilderness; every peak with "Baldy" in the name—whatever tickles your fancy. But there *are* several kinds of lists that lots of climbers choose to pursue:

- "highest" lists—for example, the 50 (or 100) highest peaks in Montana
- "highpoint" lists—for example, the highest point in each state, or in each county
- "range" lists—for example, the highest peak in each mountain range in Montana
- "biggest" lists—for example, the 50 (or 100) biggest peaks in Montana

Unfortunately, there's a sticky point in this peak-listing business:

What is a peak?

To understand the problem, visualize a basic mountain range. There are valleys and ridges. The valleys rise continuously from the adjacent plains until they eventually merge into the ridges. The ridges also rise from the adjacent plains and typically merge to form a crest and the highpoint of the range. But their rise is rarely continuous—they go up, then drop a bit, then go up some more.

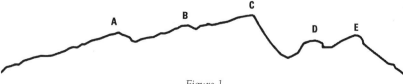

Figure 1

(*See Figure 1*) This sketch represents the profile of a hypothetical mountain ridge, with the various highpoints along that ridge labeled. The question is, which of these highpoints are peaks—worthy of a place on your list—and which are just "bumps" along the route? There is no "right" answer to this question. One possible answer is to list, as peaks, only those highpoints that have a name. However, this approach often proves unsatisfying for several reasons. First, there are many really big peaks, including some range highpoints, that have no name. Conversely, there are quite a few pretty insignificant bumps, often dwarfed by an adjacent named or nameless peak, that do have names.

Fortunately, there is an objective measure, "prominence", to help you decide which highpoints merit listing as a peak. Remember the "Four Thousand Footer Club"? Here's how the AMC describes which peaks warrant a spot on their list: "Criteria for the official list are: (1) each peak must be 4000ft in altitude, and (2) each peak must rise a clear 200 feet above the low point of its connecting ridge with a 4000 foot neighbor."

In other words, each peak must be at least 4000ft in elevation and have at least 200ft of prominence (p200).

Here are a few alternate definitions of prominence (p):
— It's the minimum elevation one must descend to get from the peak to higher terrain.
— Find the lowest contour that encircles the peak and no higher terrain. Its prominence is the difference in elevation between that contour and the summit.
— Trace every ridge that leads from the peak to higher terrain and identify the lowest point along it. The "key saddle" (sometimes called "key col") is then the highest one of those low points, and the peak's prominence is the difference in elevation between its summit and key saddle.

Figure 2 (below) illustrates a p400 standard applied to the hypothetical ridge in Figure 1.

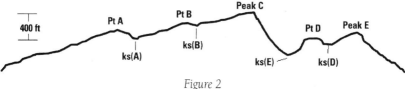

Figure 2

So, in order to construct your list of peaks, you define any specific criteria, e.g. "Baldy" in the name, and choose your prominence cutoff or standard (like p200 for the AMC list).

When I created my list of Montana peaks, I chose a standard of a minimum of 400 feet of prominence (p400) to be considered a peak, and I continue to follow that standard in this guide. I had, and have, two reasons for doing so:
(1) As the cutoff decreases, the number of peaks increases (there are many more p200 peaks than p400 peaks!), and being a "mature" climber, I wanted a reasonable number of peaks on my lists.

(2) I wanted to be able to readily determine a peak's prominence using topographic maps. In many instances, there is no spot elevation indicated on the map for a peak's key saddle and occasionally none for the peak itself; so one has to approximate their elevations using contour lines. For mountain regions those lines are generally drawn at 40 foot intervals; so the presence of at least 11 contours (400 ft) between key saddle and highpoint meant I had a peak. In contrast, a p300 standard (which is fairly common, like for the Colorado "14ers") is messier to deal with since 300 feet works out to 7½ contours.

Regardless of the standard used, there are situations when either the peak's elevation or the elevation of its key saddle (or both) is unknown, and when their difference might or might not exceed 400 feet (or whatever the standard is). This situation gives rise to two additional terms: "clean" prominence and "optimistic" prominence. Clean prominence is the minimum possible, optimistic is the maximum possible. The tables in this book list clean prominence—but I list both values when the optimistic (maximum) prominence exceeds 400 feet but the clean (minimum possible) is less than 400 feet.

One final note about prominence. It is generally quite straightforward to determine the prominence of most peaks, with one exception: the highpoint of each range. For example, Crazy Peak is the highpoint of the Crazy Mountains. One can readily find the prominence of every other peak in the range by tracing the various connecting ridges and identifying the key saddles (*see Figure 2*). But what is the prominence of Crazy Peak, or, alternatively, where is its key saddle? This can be mind-numbingly difficult to determine, especially when you look at really big & high mountains for which the higher terrain is a long way away. Fortunately, some peakbaggers are geeks, and one fellow has actually written a computer program to find any point's key saddle using digital elevation model (DEM) data.

But wait—Crazy Peak, like any range highpoint, is obviously a peak and a really big, prominent one at that. So why bother figuring out its prominence?

Naming Peaks

The Geographic Names Information System (GNIS) is the official catalog for names used on all USGS and other federal agency maps. Peakbaggers commonly defer to the GNIS usage where it exists. But what about those features, like many peaks, that have no name—i.e., aren't listed in the GNIS? There are several ways to proceed.

Some "nameless" features have widely accepted common names that occur in books and on lists but not on government maps. Examples include "Adel Mountains" for the volcanic northern end of the Big Belts and "Metcalf Mountain" for a former 12,000 foot peak in the Beartooth Mountains. (Its 'new' elevation is 11,977.)

If a peak has a bench mark on or near its summit, you can use the bench mark name. When I do this, I use all caps and include "BM." For example, the highpoint of the Ruby Mountains is RUBY BM. (see photo)

If a peak has a spot elevation for its summit, some folks use that for a name, for example "Peak 10,606," which is the highpoint of the Henrys Lake Mountains.

Because there are lists of peaks based on prominence rather than elevation (or names or geography). For example, one popular quest is to climb every peak with at least 5000 feet of prominence (there are 57 p5000 peaks in the "lower 48", and Crazy Peak is one of them). Another is to climb your state's 50 "biggest" or most prominent peaks (Crazy Peak heads the Montana list).

Where do elevations come from?

The elevations for peaks and key saddles are most commonly taken from USGS topographic maps. But if you look up a peak's elevation on different websites or different maps, you may be surprised to find different values. For example, Mount Edith has listed elevations of 9480, 9480+, 9500, 9504, and 9507 in various sources. What's going on?

There are a number of issues that complicate the seemingly straightforward matter of determining a peak's elevation:

(1) surveys, maps and databases are periodically revised;
(2) list makers deal with uncertainty in different ways;
(3) our understanding of the shape of the earth changes;
(4) the elevations are actually changing!

This section examines, in part, the first two issues. For more depth, see Appendix B (Bench marks and elevation) and Appendix C (Geodesy, Geology, and elevation).

Survey & map revisions—the "official" elevations.

Currently, the USGS 7.5 minute quadrangles, published at a scale of 1:24,000, are the standard source for determining elevations of peaks and their key saddles. Mapping of Montana's mountain areas at 1:24,000 was not completed until the mid-1990s. Before then, peakbaggers constructed lists based on data from older 15 minute maps, which have a scale of 1:62,500. Unfortunately, as a cost-saving measure, the USGS cut back on the number of spot elevations it included on the

---

Sometimes listers make up names or use existing names for nearby features. For example, the nameless highpoint of the mountain region between Flint Creek and Rock Creek (of trout fishing fame), which includes the John Long Mountains, lies at the southern end of Butte Cabin Ridge, and several listers give that name to the peak.

The approach I use in this guide is designed to reference peaks using USFS or BLM maps, without recourse to the elevations on topo maps. So I call the highpoint of the Henrys Lake Mountains "Pk S of Sheep Mtn" because it is located south of Sheep Mountain, which is indicated on the USFS map. Similarly, the highpoint of the John Long Mountains area is "Pk E of Quigg Pk." (For a really geeky approach to naming nameless peaks, see Appendix A: Using UTMs.)

newer maps. This means one often has to choose between spot elevations from the old map series, or contour elevations from the newer, larger-scale mapping.

For example, from the 15 minute map, which was published in 1950, Hilgard Peak is the highpoint of the Madison Range at 11,316 ft, ahead of 2nd place Koch Peak at 11,286 ft. From the 7.5 minute mapping, which was published in 1994 (provisional) and 2000 (final), Koch Peak is now 11,293 ft. but Hilgard Peak has no spot elevation, just a highest contour of 11,280 ft. So it's no longer clear, from the new topos, how high Hilgard Peak is and whether it's the highpoint of the range.

However, the Geographic Names Information System or GNIS (see the "naming peaks" box) used to include elevations for many named features. This database was periodically revised, and the versions starting around 1995 listed an elevation of 11,297 ft for Hilgard Peak. (More recently the Board of Geographic Names, which maintains the GNIS, decided to replace all of the surveyed elevation data in the GNIS with interpolated data from the "National Elevation Dataset"; and, unfortunately, these interpolated data are worthless.)

List-maker choices—sources and uncertainty.

Two choices were mentioned above: some list-makers prefer old but specific elevations (11,316ft) over new but uncertain values (11,280+ft); and some list-makers use only map (USGS) elevations, while some use those from the GNIS or from bench mark data when they are available (see Appendix B).

For peaks (and key saddles) with no bench mark and no elevation on the map or in the GNIS, the issue becomes: how does one list a contour elevation? Going back to Mount Edith, the topo map shows a highest contour of 9480 ft. So one choice would be to list the elevation of Mount Edith as 9480+ft. But some list-makers don't like those "+" signs. They might use '9480', or they might add half the contour interval and use '9500' (9480 + 1/2 of 40). I prefer to use the "+" sign—except Mount Edith happens to have an elevation of 9507 feet in the pre-interpolated versions of the GNIS. (I have no idea where the '9504' value comes from; it is published in the DeLorme Atlas.)

What is a mountain range?

Yet another popular quest, and my personal favorite, is to climb the highest point of every mountain range in ... you fill in the blank. But this raises yet another definitional dilemma, one that unfortunately has no simple, objective resolution like prominence is for peaks.

Some ranges are well-defined: an area filled with ridges and peaks and surrounded by plains or bounded by major rivers, and with one commonly accepted name. Examples in Montana include the Purcell Mountains, the Tobacco Root Mountains, the Big Snowy Mountains and the Pryor Mountains.

But there are many mountainous areas of the state where complex geography and/or troubled nomenclature conspire to thwart the list-maker.

The primary source of mountain range names is common or historic usage. That usage may reflect geology, topography, or hydrography; but then again, it might not. It almost never includes a clear understanding of boundaries or extent. There may be multiple names for a given area, and conversely, there are areas with no names at all. Plus the landscape itself is often confusing, with different mountain masses rising, merging, separating and disappearing in hopelessly complex patterns.

Some examples of particularly troublesome areas (and how I've delt with them) include:

(1) The boundary between the Beartooth Mountains and Absaroka Range. I use geology: the Absaroka Range includes the predominately volcanic areas while the Beartooth Mountains include the areas dominated by metamorphic rocks. [Note that most of the Absaroka Range is located in Wyoming, as is the range highpoint, Francs Peak (13,153 ft). The Montana portion of the range should really be called the "Northern Absarokas."]

(2) The boundary between the Cabinet Mountains and Salish Mountains. From around Libby all the way to the Clark Fork/Flathead River, the boundary between these two mountainous areas is unclear. Geology and topography are not much help here—it's all Belt formation rock, and the topography is quite jumbled. So I use hydrography, following the Fisher River and Little Bitterroot River. This delineation puts the Thompson Peak/Baldy Mountain area in the Cabinet Mountains. Other folks use the Thompson River as the boundary, which makes Baldy Mountain the highpoint of the Salish Mountains. But the USGS topographic map does have a "Cabinet Mountains" label on Corona Ridge, just NE of Baldy Mountain.

(3) The area along the continental divide between McDonald Pass and Rogers Pass. There is no commonly accepted name for this area. Some folks extend the boundaries of the Garnet Range eastward to include the divide north of McDonald Pass. Forest Service maps show the Lewis & Clark Range extending a bit southeast of Rogers Pass. And some sources have the Boulder Mountains extending a bit north of McDonald Pass. But I prefer to let the area stand alone, as the "Nevada Mountain area."

There is occasional confusion over the use of "range" versus "mountains." For example, the Missions are officially the Mission Range; but the high country is all within the tribal and federal "Mission Mountains Wilderness" areas. Note too that "Bitterroot Range", as used on USGS and FS maps, denotes the long divide (and Idaho-Montana state line) from the mouth of the Clark Fork River at Lake Pend d'Oreille south and east to Monida Pass on I-15 (and including the Coeur d'Alene and Beaverhead Mountains). "Bitterroot Mountains" refers to that portion of the Bitterroot Range located between Lookout Pass and Lost Trail Pass.

The Bitterroot and Beaverhead Mountains are both very long ranges that change character significantly along their length. So in this guide I have divided the Bitterroot Mountains into the main "Bitterroots" and "Northern Bitterroots" at Lolo Pass, based on stature and geology. The Northern Bitterroots are 2000 feet lower than the main Bitterroots and primarily Belt formation rather than granite. I also split off the northern portion of the Beaverhead Mountains (north of Lemhi Pass) as the "West Big Hole", based on geology and topography.

The map and tables on pages 132-134 present Montana's mountain ranges (as used in this guide) and their highpoints, along with a table of "subranges"—named ranges that I have lumped with a larger, "parent" range—and their highpoints.

Close Calls

Though most ranges have an undisputed highpoint—a peak that soars above all others in the range—several have two peaks that are quite close in elevation, and for two ranges there are serious questions about which of two peaks rules. The following table presents a list of the close calls.

RANGE	HP# 1	HP#2
Big Snowies	Greathouse Peak (8,681)	Old Baldy (8,680+)
Pryors	Big Pryor Mountain (8,786)	East Pryor Mountain (8,776)
Elkhorns	Crow Peak (9,415)	Elkhorn Peak (9,400+)
Madison	Hilgard Peak (11,297)	Koch Peak (11,293)
East Pioneers	Tweedy Mountain (11,154)	Torrey Mountain (11,147)
Snowcrest	Sunset Peak (10,581)	Hogback Peak (10,572)
Thompson Peak area	Baldy Mountain (7,464)	Thompson Peak (7,460)

I suspect that Old Baldy is actually the highpoint of the Big Snowies, and I highly recommend you climb them both. Old Baldy has a tiny closed contour at 8680ft. BIG SNOWY BM, which is on Old Baldy, has an elevation of 8678 but is visibly 3-4 feet lower than the highest point. That would put Old Baldy's elevation at 8681+—equal to or higher than the elevation for Greathouse Peak.

For the Pryors we actually have conflicting data and not just a lack of data, as displayed below. Again, the prudent peakbagger will visit all three highpoints. (See Appendices B and C for an explanation of the terms in this table.)

Peak	BM	USGS (topos/ GNIS)	NGS NGVD29	NGS NAVD88	Notes
East Pryor Mtn	ICE	8,776	8,787	8,791	on highest point
Big Pryor Mtn-NW	SHRIVER	8,780	8,787	8,790	not on highest point
Big a Mtn	ICE CAVE	8,786	-na-	8,789	on highest point

In the Elkhorns, Crow is generally acknowledged to be the higher peak; but there are no current data to substantiate that, just data from the old 15 minute mapping.

As for the rest, the data clearly favor one peak over its runner-up. But given how small the differences are and how these measurements and data can change over time, it might be worth bagging their runners-up too!

Baldy Lake Basin from Baldy Mountain, Cabinet Mountains.

Resources

There are many excellent online and print resources that address different aspects of peakbagging, from geology and prominence theory to detailed route descriptions for hundreds of different peaks. In the "Routes" section of this guide I identify specific books and websites that have information about each peak. The lists below describe those sources and several others I find particularly useful.

Books

The obvious drawback to books is that the information they present is static—a snapshot of conditions at one point in time. But sometimes that historic information can be useful (like documenting an abandoned trail or a now-forgotten route), and sometimes it's just nice to relax with a book and do some armchair mountaineering. The books listed below are ordered by the codes or abbreviations I use in the "Routes" section. They are included here because they contain information pertaining to at least one of the peaks featured in this guide.

AIRG   *Alpine Ice & Rock Guide to Southwest and Central Montana*. 2000. Ron Brunckhorst

B-B   *Bitterroot to Beartooth*. 1985. Ruth Rudner

CGGNP   *Climbers Guide to Glacier National Park*. 1995. J Gordon Edwards
This edition is much better than the original 1976 edition and definitely worth reading before any attempt on a peak in the Park.

CGM   *Climbers Guide to Montana*. 1986. Pat Caffrey.
This book is out-of-print and may be hard to find. It contains actual route descriptions for only a few peaks, and those tend to be cryptic or brief. But I always check my copy before going to an area I don't know well.

DRMF   *Discover the Rocky Mountain Front: A Hiking Guide*. 2006. Tom Kotynski.

EIM   *Exploring Idaho's Mountains: A Guide for Climbers, Scramblers & Hikers*. 1990. Tom Lopez.
This book is directly relevant for only those peaks that lie on the Montana-Idaho state line. But it is such a good guide—encyclopedic, informative, concise— and Idaho has so many wonderful peaks too, that you really should get hold of one.

HAB   *Day Hikes Around Bozeman*. 2001. Robert Stone.

HGM79   *The Hiker's Guide to Montana*. 1979. Bill Schneider.

HGM94   *The Hiker's Guide to Montana: 4th Edition*. 1994. Bill Schneider.

HM04   *Hiking Montana: 25th Anniversary Edition*. 2004. Bill & Russ Schneider.

HYNP   *Hiking Yellowstone National Park*. 1997. Bill Schneider.

SPGY   *Select Peaks of Greater Yellowstone: A Mountaineering History & Guide*. 2003. Thomas Turiano.
This is a wonderful book—combination of coffee-table book/climbing guide—detailed and interesting information about the peaks it covers.

WM   *Wild Montana*. 1995. Bill Cunningham.
An excellent source for many lesser-known areas of the state.

-na-   *Islands on the Prairie: Eastern Montana's Mountain Ranges*. 1986. Mark Meloy. Primarily a picture book, with no peak or route information, it is still worth perusing for ideas of places to explore.

Websites

Wikipedia article on topographic prominence.
http://en.wikipedia.org/wiki/ Topographic_prominence
The article on topographic prominence in Wikipedia provides a good basic overview of the concept and its application, plus many useful links.

National Geodetic Survey (NGS) datasheets.
http://www.ngs.noaa.gov/cgi-bin/datasheet.prl
This NGS page provides access to information about individual bench marks, including current location, elevation and history.

Geographic Names Information System (GNIS). http://geonames.usgs.gov/
Online searching for names in the GNIS; for peaks choose CLASS = "summit." But remember that the elevations listed are from the "National Elevation Dataset" and are generally worthless.

Peakbagger.com. http://www.peakbagger.com/
Besides a huge and diverse selection of peak lists, and tools for registered users to track and share their climbs, this site offers a world-wide "taxonomy" or classification/naming system for mountain ranges. And the peak list pages provide links to pages on individual peaks, with information on location, key saddle and prominence, plus an on-line topo map of the peak.

Peaklist.org. http://www.peaklist.org/
Another site with a huge selection of lists — but the focus is on world-wide prominence lists. Also has in-depth articles about prominence theory.

Looking northeast from the basin below the east peak of Rocky Mountain, Sawtooth Range.

Lists of John (Kirk). http://www.listsofjohn.com/index.html
This site provides incredible depth on US peaks — lists for every peak in every county, and for every peak on every USGS quadrangle, plus peak pages with map links and often a photo. "Members" (register on-line) can track and share their climbs and post trip reports and photos.

Summitpost. http://www.summitpost.org/
The preeminent site for trip reports for peaks all over the world (including Montana). Also includes background information and photos for many peaks, plus some peak lists and information on mountain ranges. Summitpost is my first stop when I plan to climb a peak that's new to me.

County Highpointers Association. http://www.cohp.org/
Lists for the entire US, trip reports, background information, and many good links. You can register and use on-line tools to keep track of and share your "highpointing" exploits. (Click "trip reports" in the map graphic, then select the state and county.)

MyTopo.com. http://www.mytopo.com/maps.cfm
This is currently the easiest site to use for perusing topographic maps of an area. You can zoom in either by searching for a GNIS named feature or from an interactive mapping tool.

Google Maps. http://maps.google.com/
This interactive mapping tool lets you quickly zoom in to satellite imagery of any place in the US. You can find your house, or figure out potential routes to and on a peak. Note that Google Earth provides the same imagery but with really nifty viewing tools.

Beartooth Publishing. http://www.beartoothpublishing.com/index.php
Produced high-quality trail maps for certain areas around the state, especially the Beartooth Mountains and Yellowstone NP. Maps include suggested/featured hikes and mountain bike rides.

Rocky Mountaineers. http://www.rockymountaineers.com/rmcms/
A Missoula-based outdoor club that does frequent mountain trips and publishes a monthly newsletter that often contains good trip reports.

Custer National Forest. http://www.fs.fed.us/r1/custer/recreation/granitepeak.shtml
The Custer National Forest has a page about climbing Granite Peak, with detailed information for the standard route and its two most common approaches.

Safety and peakbagging tips

"We get too soon old and too late smart" *(old Yiddish saying)*
The ultimate cause of death may be birth, but there are proximate causes you may want to avoid, especially while peakbagging, such as lightning, hypothermia, and falling.

To climb safely you need judgment, self-control, and competence:

• Judgment—to assess your abilities versus the demands and risks of the situation.

• Self-control—to think things through and not panic when events don't go as planned.

• Competence—to plan and prepare for your climb and to expand your options if things go wrong.

Part of competence is knowing stuff—knowing what to take, knowing how to climb, knowing how to navigate with map and compass or GPS. Part of competence is efficiency—saving time and energy by moving efficiently across the landscape. And part of competence is paying attention—noting features on the landscape, changes in the weather, how you and your companions are faring.

Here is a grab-bag of tips to be a more competent climber:

• When going uphill, push off from your heel.

• Keep a steady pace.

• Many small steps are less tiring than few big ones.

• Learn to find and follow old, abandoned trails—they save time & energy.

• Learn to find and follow game trails—they save time & energy.

• It's often harder to stay on route going down than going up: you're moving faster, you're tired and not as focused, and topology is against you (routes converge going up but diverge going down). Pay attention!

• Look back at key junctures and make cairns (but be sure to knock them over on your way out).

• Avoid rubble (small talus) and large talus (rocks bigger than motorcycles): both are slow, tiring and tiresome. Try to stay on rocks from 1-4 feet across: they're big enough to be stable but small enough to easily step from one to the next.

• The color and texture of veg varies with how wet the ground is. Look for the differences and try to stay on dry ground—it's much easier walking (less impact too).

• When your route starts getting steep and hairy, remember to always zig before you zag (i.e., zig-zag).

• Carry map and compass and know how to use them. (NOTE: I've never used a GPS for hiking, so obviously you won't find any coordinate data for the routes in this book—just cardinal directions.)

• Especially when hiking in a new area, stop often to read the map and landscape together. A given pattern of contours can mean a fun climb, a total no-go, or a tiresome slog depending on geology, aspect, climate and other variables.

- And finally, large, potentially dangerous animals inhabit many mountainous areas in Montana. Learn how to travel safely in their country and what to do if you encounter them.

Avoiding lightening and hypothermia is generally a matter of judgment, but moving efficiently and saving time and energy so you're off the mountain before thunderstorms develop and/or darkness falls can greatly reduce your exposure to these risks.

Only a few of the routes described in this guide present a risk of falling, but many **mountains** in this guide do; so stay on route. Most falls occur in panic situations: you're descending, it's late, you're tired, you get off route, you panic and try to make it go.

View of Glacier National Park from Great Northern Mountain, Flathead Range.

Mount Jefferson, Centennial Mountains.

Route descriptions

The most difficult part of this project for me was deciding which peaks to include and which routes on those peaks to describe in detail. My database of Montana peaks includes almost 3000 p400 peaks, just over 700 p1000s, and 147 p2000s. The lists in this book include about 200 unique peaks. Since my primary intent with this guide is to introduce hikers to peakbagging, I want to provide fairly detailed directions on finding and climbing the peaks. That means selecting a manageable (for me) number of those peaks to focus on.

I selected peaks for their status from a peakbagger's perspective, their access, their aesthetics, how thoroughly they are treated in other sources, and geographic and landscape diversity. I constrained myself to routes accessible by a 2WD vehicle and tended to chose the shortest and easiest—though aesthetics factored in.

Listed below are the kinds of routes described in this guide with examples of peaks in each catagory.

(1) Routes entirely on trail
    Northwest Peak
    McGuire Mountain
    Baldy Mountain (Plains)
    Sacagawea Peak
    Big Baldy Mountain
    Greathouse Peak
(2) Routes with short and easy bushwhacking
    Ch-paa-qn Peak
    Mount Edith
(3) Routes with significant bushwhacking
    QUARTZ BM
    McLeod Peak
    McDonald Peak
    RUBY BM
(4) Routes with short and easy scrambling
    Haystack Mountain
    Elk Peak
(5) Peaks with optional scrambling
    Mount Jefferson
    Homer Youngs Peak
(6) Peaks that require 3rd class scrambling
    Hilgard Peak
    Mount Cowen
    Granite Peak
    Crazy Peak (due to access constraints)
(7) Peaks generally requiring multiple days
    Kintla Peak
    Mount Cleveland
    Mount Stimson
    Mount Wood
    Castle Mountain
    Granite Peak
    Mount Cowen

Some notes about the descriptions:

Online and digital sources of topographic mapping are now so ubiquitous that I am providing only small locator and overview maps in this guide. They may well suffice for the easy peaks; but for longer and more difficult climbs you should use a topographic map.

I give one-way mileages and elevation gain for 'in & out' routes, but round-trip figures for loops.

I've tried to select routes that are fun and interesting for hikers who may be afraid of heights or could care less about climbing a mountain.

Difficulty is hard to assess. I provide the basic distance and elevation data and a brief note about how tough the country is, but those often fail to adequately describe a route's physical and psychological demands. In addition, "conditions", such as the weather, is there snow or muddy/boggy ground, has the trail been recently cleared or is it choked with brush and downfall, how competent and prepared are you and your companions, can vary widely and can significantly affect a route's difficulty. Nevertheless, after doing a few of these routes you should hopefully be able to calibrate your abilities against my descriptions.

Speaking of 'conditions', central and southwest Montana is currently (2010) experiencing two major insect epidemics. The mountain pine beetle is killing off many ponderosa, lodgepole and whitebark pines, and the spruce budworm is killing many Douglas fir. If they don't burn in the next few years all these dead trees will eventually become deadfall—stressing trail maintenance budgets and adding, in places, to the considerable deadfall remaining from the 1930s beetle epidemic. What are now pleasant routes through mostly open woods could become high-stepping nightmares in a few years.

Sacagawea Peak (center) and Hardscrabble Peak (in sun) from Cottonwood Reservoir north of Wilsall.

Antoine Butte (5,720+ft — p 2,670ft)

Status
> Highpoint of the Little Rocky Mountains
> Phillips County HP & BP
> Prominence rank = 70

Difficulty
> Day hike mostly on roads
> 4.5 miles one-way with 2000ft gain
> Parts of this route are on private land

Other sources
> Website: County Highpointers

Land status
> BLM & private

The Little Rockies were home to two huge gold mines, one of which was centered in Ruby Gulch above the town of Zortman and on the slopes of Antoine Butte. Though the landscape is far from pristine, pockets of great beauty remain, and the big views are strangely attractive. It's worth the effort to visit and climb this peak and Old Scraggy.

Driving

Two county roads lead from US 191 to Zortman; they intersect about 1/2 mile east of town. (From that junction it's a long mile north to the lovely, and birdy, BLM campground along Camp Creek.) Just as you start to enter Zortman, take a road branching left that winds around some houses and heads west up Alder Gulch. Park in an open area about 1/2 mile up this road, where an eroded track drops down from the north.

Antoine Butte (left horizon) from Old Scraggy.

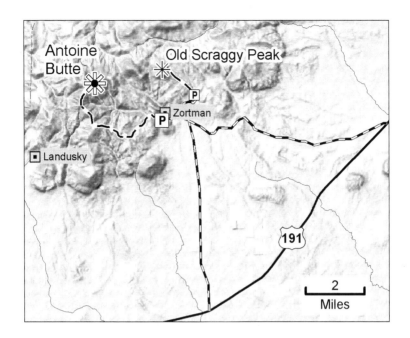

Route

Walk up the road, partly in the creek, to a fork. Go left (the right branch up Alder Gulch is posted a short ways up) and head up Pony Gulch. Pass a newer road branching left in about 1/3 mile and continue up a badly eroded stretch to a ridge. Follow the main road generally W to NW along the ridge—it's woodsy on the north, open with views on the south. It ends at a big berm that blocks vehicle access to a wide, graveled mining road. Follow this road (expect some traffic) north for about 1 mile to the summit, which is the first (SW) of two tower-laden blips. There are occasional views through the extensive lodgepole pine; the best views are from the NE blip.

Old Scraggy Peak (5,708ft — p 630ft)

It's a delightful though too-short hike up second-highest Old Scraggy from the BLM campground. From the north end of the campground loop, an ATV track leads up to the main "Beaver Creek Road". You can turn right and follow the road as it climbs east to a ridge and loops around to the NE side of Old Scraggy. You can also turn left, cross Camp Creek and then head north on an old track that climbs directly towards the peak. This track traverses the east side of the peak, then drops slightly to rejoin the Beaver Creek Road. From its highpoint just south of that junction, a short, steep bushwhack through dog-hair lodgepole pine leads to the rocky outcrops of the summit and some fascinating views.

Baldy Mountain (7,464ft — p 4,064ft)

Status
    Highpoint of the Thompson Peak area
    Prominence rank = 13

Difficulty
    Half-day hike on trail
    2+ miles one-way with 2100ft gain

Other sources
    - none

Land status
    Lolo NF

Baldy is at the southern end of one of the Salish-Cabinet sub-ranges, a big pile of rubble looming over the town of Plains. It used to have a lookout tower on top and a small ski area on its lower slopes. The view is still incredible, but with its flat summit and small trees, one has to walk around a bit to see it all. The trail starts out in somewhat decadent woods, but gets more interesting the higher one goes and passes by some wonderfully gnarly old trees.

Old snags above the Clark Fork valley, slopes of Baldy Mountain.

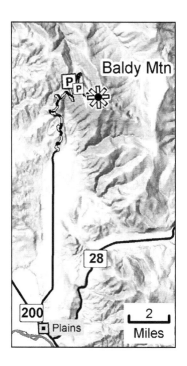

Baldy is only 4 feet higher than Thompson Peak, which is plainly visible about 10 miles to the north. (Thompson is another old lookout site, well-served by trails and with no views except from the rocky summit. The shortest hike is from the Little Thompson River and FS roads 519 & 5582.)

Driving

In Plains, head north on Clayton Street past the FS Ranger Station. It turns into Upper Lynch Creek Road, which is paved. Turn left onto "Corona Road" at the sign 9 miles north of town and follow this good gravel road 4+ miles to a 'hiker' sign on a road branching right, immediately after a tight switchback. 2.5 miles up this road, just past another road branching left (that drops to Corona Lake and the old ski area) park in a wide spot on the left (NW) side of the road, across from another unobtrusive 'hiker' sign, at 5400ft. NOTE: there is another trailhead an additional mile or so further up; but even the lower trailhead is a lot of driving for not that much hiking.

Route

Hike up the gentle trail to the top. Expect some loose rock where the trail crosses open rubble slopes. Be sure to walk over to the SE edge of the summit for a view of the Baldy Lake basin.

Bearpaw Baldy (6,916ft — p 4,226ft)
(GNIS name = Baldy Mountain)

Status
> Highpoint of the Bears Paw Mountains
> Prominence rank = 11
> Hill County HP & BP

Difficulty
> Half-day hike on primitive trail
> 2 miles one-way with 2100ft gain
> Trail is hard to find and follow, and portions are quite steep

Other sources
> Websites: County Highpointers
> Books: HGM 79&94

Land status
> Chippewa-Cree Tribal land

The Bearpaws are a small range of rounded hills with many isolated buttes trailing off to the east. They are at their best when spring wildflowers or fall foliage color the hills. The range is almost entirely either tribal or private land, so access is not a given but varies over time and location.

Driving

From Havre, go up lovely Beaver Creek Rd (MT 234) about 30 miles (all paved) to a dirt road branching left, signed "Eagle Creek", at 4800ft.

From Box Elder on US 87, turn east towards Rocky Boy Agency. After a mile or so, turn left at a Chippewa-Cree sign and head up Box Elder Creek to a "T" just past the reservoir. Turn right for Rocky Boy Agency and then, in town, turn left (east) by Stone Child College and head over the pass to Beaver Creek (with 2 miles of dirt road that could be dicey when wet). You'll hit Beaver Creek Rd about 20 miles from US 87 and about 9 miles below (north of) the "Eagle Creek" road.

Bearpaw Baldy from the north.

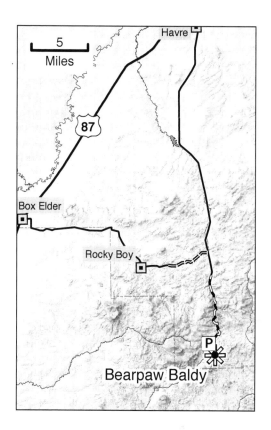

Route

The best way up is to follow the old trail. Even though it's not a constructed or maintained trail (i.e., no blazes, no cut-out deadfall), its well-worn tread provides the best route, especially up high in the rubble. There are just two problems: finding the trail and then staying on it.

To find the trail, drop SE from the Ironmaker Camp (about 100 yards up the road), cross Eagle Creek (which drains the basin between Baldy and Wellen Peak) and climb east through woods and a logged area to the crest of a ridge. Head south up the ridge, picking up (if you haven't already) an old fence line. The trail follows the fence (or visa-versa) up the ridge, which is narrow and scenic, then traverses the east side of a small, rocky blip into a grassy saddle at the base of the mountain. The fence, and trail, head straight up—but soon the now fairly-obvious trail crosses to the NE side of the fence and wiggles its way up through the woods, soon breaking out into open slopes of grass and rubble. (A 'wiggle' is like a switchback, only much smaller and steeper.) At one point it switchbacks left then right to gain the top of a short cliff, but mostly it wiggles straight for the top. About 200 feet below the top, it makes a long, gentle traverse over to the south ridge of the peak, just a short, mostly grassy walk below the open summit.

On the descent it's easier to lose the trail—so go slowly and pay attention! There are old cairns in the rubble section that mark the route, but they can be hard to see.

Big Baldy Mountain (9,177ft — p 3,557ft)

Status

Highpoint of the Little Belt Mountains
Prominence rank = 33
Judith Basin County HP & BP

Difficulty

A long trail hike (open to motorcycles)
9 miles one-way with 3300ft gain
Trails mostly obvious—somewhat rubbly up high

Other sources

Websites: County Highpointers

Land status

Lewis & Clark NF

The Little Belts are a very large range of mostly very gentle mountains, with lots of forest, logging and logging roads, and motorized recreation. But there are areas with much to offer the hiker—especially the many fine limestone canyons all about the fringes of the range and up the Middle Fork Judith River. It's slimmer pickings for the peakbagger, but Barker Mountain and several other peaks along the northern edge are fun hikes, and the east side of Big Baldy is really special. Here you'll find large glacial cirques cut into a tundra plateau—a tiny bit of the Beartooths in central Montana.

Driving

From the west edge of Stanford on MT 3 & 200, turn SW onto Running Wolf Rd and follow the FS signs to Dry Wolf Campground. It's 20 miles of scenic and good gravel road. The trailhead is at the far (S) end of the campground at 5900ft.

Route

Head up trail #401 along the creek about a mile, until it climbs to a huge meadow on a bench above the creek. If the water level permits, drop down to the ford and follow the trail to a signed junction in a smaller meadow. If the water is too high, follow the rim/meadow edge south until you cut trail #402 or a logging track in the woods. A bit further south on this trail you'll find a cut-across trail (#401-A) that drops to a bridge then continues through woods to that signed junction.

Continue up Dry Wolf Creek, passing through the aftermath of an incredible micro-burst, to the junction with trail #414. (NOTE: this trail is shown correctly on

The northern cirque on Big Baldy Mountain.

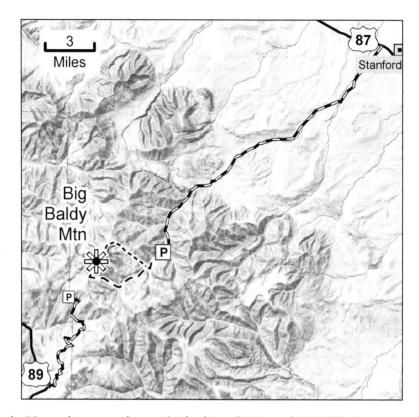

the FS map, but not on the topo.) Take this trail up towards Big Baldy. You can follow it to the saddle and then take trail #416 north, or you can leave it and head straight up through open woods and rubble slopes to the lovely tundra area on the gentle summit plateau. A small communications shed marks the summit, right on the edge of the southern cirque.

If you're comfortable with traveling over talus and navigating through trackless woods, you might consider an alternative descent. Continue north across the plateau, staying on the east rim and enjoying views of the more-precipitous northern cirque. Follow the rim around, dropping SE through talus back into the forest. Continue down on a bearing a bit north of SE, either dropping into a drainage on your right or one on your left (better) or staying on the ridge between them. All three routes lead back to that small meadow with the signed junction just south of the ford.

Alternate route
There is a short, half-day route up the SW side of the peak. It starts from FS road #3328, which leaves US 89 about 2 miles north of Kings Hill and winds north along the west side of the main divide. You can park almost anywhere from the Jefferson Creek TH on north, head east or NE up to the divide, and follow road & trail to the top.

Big Snowy Mountains HP
(8,680+ft — p 4,060+ft)

Status
>Highpoint of the Big Snowy Mountains
>Fergus County HP & BP
>Prominence rank = 14

Difficulty
>A long day hike, mostly on trail and jeep trail
>16 miles RT with 4700ft gain
>Many stream crossings—wait for low water

Other sources
>Websites: County Highpointers
>Books: HGM79

Land status
>Lewis & Clark NF

The Big Snowies are a big limy blister that's cut by long, wooded canyons on its north side and short, open canyons on the south. The eastern end of the uplift is the high ground and, as discussed under 'close calls', two peaks vie for the highpoint. Greathouse Peak and Old Baldy look at each other across Half Moon Pass at the head of Swimming Woman Canyon on the south and Half Moon Canyon on the north. The saddle and Greathouse Peak are both reached by trails up the canyons, and Old Baldy was once reached by now-closed jeep trails from the east.

Both peaks can be climbed in a day from either side, and although the Swimming Woman hike is shorter, I prefer wild & woolly Half Moon Canyon—so that's the route described below.

Driving

From Lewistown, head south on Red Hill Road for 23+ miles (the first 11 miles are paved) to the "Uhlhorn Trailhead" for Half Moon Canyon at 5600ft.

Route

This is a counter-clockwise loop: up Half Moon Canyon to Greathouse (7+ miles, mostly trail), traverse through the pass and up to Old Baldy (2+ miles off-trail), then down its NE ridge, partly on jeep trail, back to the trail and your vehicle (6+ miles).

The fairly new trailhead and trail avoids private land at the mouth of the canyon; it's about 1/2 mile over to the canyon, where you pick up the old road and follow it a very scenic 1/2 mile. The trail then continues up the bottom through thick spruce woods with many more creek crossings (up to 14 depending on water levels) before breaking out into lovely meadow country about 4 miles up at 6500ft. If you lose the trail in the big meadow where the creek forks, just head up the south side of the west branch and you'll pick it up again. Where the trail turns south to head for Half Moon Pass, continue west and pick a route up the headwall to the plateau and Greathouse Peak.

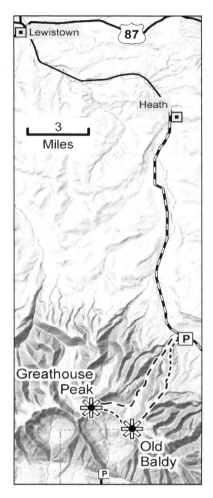

(top) *View down Half Moon Canyon from slopes of Old Baldy.*
(bottom) *Greathouse Peak beyond Half Moon Pass from north ridge of Old Baldy.*

Climb Old Baldy by following the divide through Half Moon Pass, often accompanied by a fence line. It's not as hard as it looks due to reasonable game trails, especially in the rubble slopes leading up to Old Baldy.

You'll pick up the old jeep road (now an ATV route) once you start down the NE ridge along the canyon rim. Follow it until it turns right and starts dropping off the rim into the woods. Continue along the rim, with an occasional gnarly stretch in dense conifers, until you're above the neat cliffs on the canyons east wall; then drop NE to intercept the trail and return to your vehicle.

Black Mountain (8,330ft — p 2,530ft)

Status
>Highpoint of the Nevada Mountain area
>Prominence rank = 82

Difficulty
>Day hike on trail and abandoned trail
>6 miles one way with 3500ft gain for Black Mountain;
>add another 2 miles one way with 1200ft gain for Nevada
>One section has bad deadfall—rest is OK

Other sources
>- none

Land status
>Helena NF

The country between MacDonald Pass and Rogers Pass is really kind of dull, and with all the dead and dying trees from pine beetles and spruce budworm, it's looking pretty scruffy. But there is still some very nice hiking here, and some areas that are quite scenic. Two gentle, wooded peaks dominate the area: Black Mountain and Nevada Mountain. Black is higher (8330ft vs 8293ft), but Nevada is more scenic and affords some views, and the stretch of CDT between them is the scenic highlight of the area.

The *easy* way to 'bag' Black Mountain is to drive up out of Marysville to the CDT trailhead on its SE flank and walk a couple of miles of old track/ATV trail to the top The *best* way to climb it is with two vehicles and a key exchange: one party starts as above, the other drives up Marsh Creek to the divide then south about a mile to a gate. There's a mile or two of ATV trail on either end, but the section from Black Mountain to the saddle at the head of Nevada Creek is lovely hiking.

But to really experience this area *and* get a serious workout and a dose of adventure, follow the directions below.

Driving

A bit west of the Canyon Creek store on MT 279 (Lincoln Road), turn west onto Little Prickly Pear Road and drive up the pretty valley with Nevada Mountain looming at its head. After 5.4 miles the Marsh Creek road takes off to the right and heads up to the divide—but you continue straight another 2.6 miles and turn left onto the Lost Horse Creek Road. About 2 miles up this road you round a bend and get your first view of Black Mountain, looming at the head of Deadman Creek. Turn right onto the unsigned Deadman Creek road and veer right again in 1/2 mile onto road 774 A1. Follow this slow, pot-holey road past some cabins and through a logged area (on private land). The road dips through a huge puddle and fords the creek three times. You need to park just before the last ford, if you haven't parked already (I park just before the big puddle, which is only 1/2 mile from the 3rd ford.)

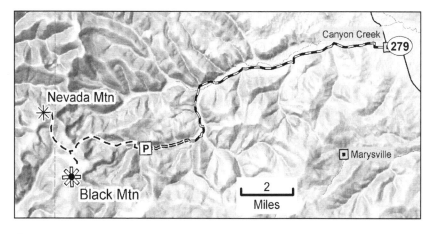

View up Deadman Creek to Black Mountain.

Route

There are actually logs a bit above or below the big puddle and the fords if you care to search them out. Immediately across the last ford, the road heads upstream but you take the barely discernible trail downstream right near the creek. Within a hundred feet it climbs the low bench and swings around to head towards the divide. Look for old FS blazes and cut logs as you continue up the trail—there is often no discernible tread, especially lower down. But it does get better the higher you go, and overall it's still a trail hike, not a bushwhack. Do expect some bad deadfall where the trail tops out on the ridge between Deadman and Beartrap creeks.

From the junction with the CDT, it's about two miles south to Black Mountain and two miles north to Nevada Mountain. On Black Mountain the ATVs have a track almost to the top on the south slope—but the summit is just an easy 10 minute bushwhack west from the CDT highpoint. Nevada Mountain is about a 20 minute bushwhack west through open woods from the CDT highpoint.

Castle Mountain (12,612ft — p 2,652ft)

Status
> Carbon County HP
> Elevation rank = 3
> Prominence rank = 72

Difficulty
> Multi-day trip with cross-country travel
> Fair amount of high-elevation talus, possibly some steep snow

Other sources
> Websites: Summitpost, County Highpointers
> Books: SPGY

Land status
> Custer NF, Absaroka-Beartooth Wilderness

Castle Mountain can be approached from the south or the east. The southern approach is much longer and the trail to Green Lake is tough—lots of up & down and boggy sections; but the climb is straightforward. The eastern approach via the West Fork of Rock Creek is much better—a short day on excellent trail. But the climb up to Omega Pass either requires ice axe and possibly crampons when there's snow, or involves 1400 ft of tiresome rubble and talus when there's not.

For the southern approach consider going via Becker and Jasper Lakes, then cross country to base camp at Flat Rock Lake. It will take two days, but it's much nicer than the trail.

For the eastern approach, read on.

Castle Mountain from lower Silt Lake, Omega Pass on left.

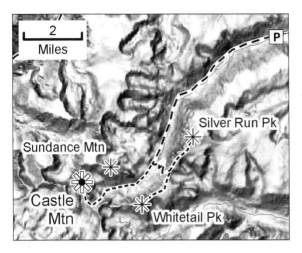

Driving

From the south edge of Red Lodge head west on the W Fk Road (the turn is poorly marked; it's N of the Ranger Station) and continue up the creek 7.5 miles on paved road to Basin Campground and another 5.5 miles on rebuilt gravel road (in 2010) through the 2008 burn to the end of the road and TH at 7900ft.

Route

Hike up the trail about 7 miles, past the side trail to Lake Mary, to the bridge over the West Fork. The first couple of miles are in burn, but the scenery practically the whole way is stunning. There are places to camp 1/4 mile before the bridge (if you're hanging food) and 100 yards past the bridge or 200 yards upstream (if you have a bear canister).

A climber's trail, occasionally ill-defined, goes up the north side of the creek to the first Silt Lake. Continue up the drainage to the flats at 10,100' (camping), then pick your route—steep snow or talus—up to Omega Pass. From the pass, head N up the ridge. At the buttress, traverse on the west side until you find a route up you're comfortable with, then walk & hop up the plateau to the top.

Other Peaks

The bridge over the west fork is a good base for three other 12,000 footers: 4th highest Whitetail Peak (12,551ft), 5th highest Silver Run Peak (12,542ft), and 16th highest Sundance Mountain (12,262ft). For the first two, hike up to Sundance Pass: the trail may be ugly to look at, but it's a delight to walk. From the pass, head NE up the plateau on veg then easy talus to the west (higher) summit of Silver Run Peak and a tremendous view down its W face. Or follow a climber's trail SW, over a blip to some veg and tougher talus up Mount Lockhart, then a short drop to the base of Whitetail Peak. Head up steep rock/talus, drop to the notch at the head of the snow couloir, traverse left to the groove on the south face (easy 3rd class) and scramble on up.

For Sundance Mountain, look for and follow a climber's trail that takes off W about 200 ft before (N of) the bridge and climbs towards Ship Lake. Head cross-country up the meadowy ridge to the base of the NE rib, and take your choice of steep snow or steep rock to the plateau and summit.

Chalk Buttes HP (4,200+ft — p 720ft)

Status
Highpoint of the Long Pines area
Carter County BP

Difficulty
Half-day hike on road and cross-country
6 miles RT with 800ft gain

Other sources
- none

Land status
Custer NF

The Forest Service manages three small areas of Ponderosa Pine-covered sandstone plateaus south of Ekalaka: the Chalk Buttes, the Ekalaka Hills, and the Long Pines. This really isn't peak-bagging country. The "highpoints" of all three areas are barely perceptible, and roads run over much of the high ground. But it's worth including the Chalk Buttes HP in this guide for several reasons. First, the location and setting in extreme SE Montana is unique. Second, the scenery is unique and, in the Chalk Buttes, really spectacular. Third, although a jeep road does gain the main plateau, vehicle use appears minimal and does not detract from the primitive feel of the area. And finally, the Chalk Buttes HP is, by 80 feet or so, the highest point in the entire area and a nice hike to boot.

White sandstone cliffs above Trenk Pass.

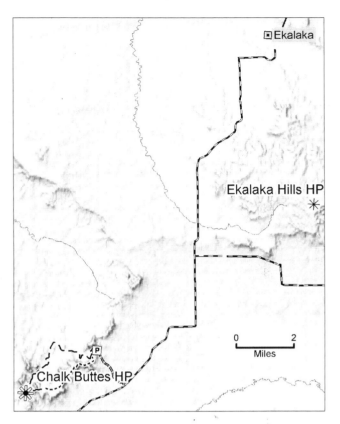

Driving

In Ekalaka, find Central St. (a few blocks west of S. Main) and head south—it becomes Chalk Buttes Rd. About 10 miles S of town you'll drive past Pershing Cutoff Rd on the left (east); continue generally south another 6.3 miles to the FS Chalk Buttes access road on the right. Take this road, badly water-damaged in 2010, about 1.8 miles up to the NF boundary. Park here or 200 yds further at Trenk Pass.

From US 212 in Alzada or Hammond, go north towards Ekalaka to the sign for Pershing Cutoff Rd on MT 323, head west about 10 miles to Chalk Buttes Rd and proceed as above.

Route

The highpoint is at the extreme SW corner of the NF land and the plateau. The road loops around on the NW side of the plateau then climbs to a saddle that's about 200 yds NE of the highpoint, between it and the main plateau, before heading E up to the plateau and disappearing in the grasses. That's one leg of your loop. The other is to cross the plateau (mostly prairie with scattered Ponderosa pine), continue E across a "narrows" to a final bit of plateau, then drop N or NE to the road and back up to Trenk Pass. A compass (or GPS) could be helpful in navigating the extensive prairie on top. Don't drop off the plateau until you can see the neat butte N of Trenk Pass.

Ch-paa-qn Peak (7,996ft — p 3,996ft)

Status
> Highpoint of the Reservation Divide and Ninemile Creek mountains
> Prominence rank = 16 or 17
> possibly Missoula County BP (tied with Holland Peak)

Difficulty
> Half-day hike on trail
> 3-3.5 miles one-way with 1800-2300ft gain
> The trail quits a bit below the top on a gentle talus slope

Other sources
> Websites: Summitpost
> Books: WM, CGM

Land status
> Lolo NF

Ch-paa-qn used to be Squaw Peak but got its new name following passage of a law in 1999 mandating the elimination of "squaw" from Montana place names (see: MCA 2-15-149). There are three approaches to the mountain, two of which offer half-day hikes. One is via the Edith Peak road (#476) and trail #98 along the divide; the other is via Butler Creek road (#456) and trail #707 up the ridge between Butler and Stony creeks. The divide route is gentler and a bit more scenic, but both can be combined if you have two vehicles and do a key exchange or shuttle. The hiking is pleasant but not that special—one climbs this peak for the incredible view (and to 'bag' it!).

Ladybugs in summit talus.

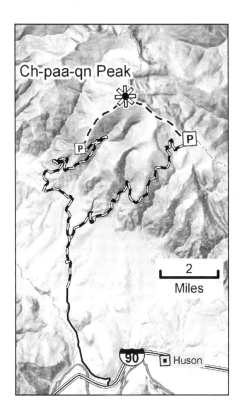

Driving

From exit 82 on I-90, follow signs to the historic Ninemile Ranger Station. Continue north on the Edith Peak road another 10 miles to the divide and trailhead at 6235ft.

For trail #707, branch left onto road #456 about 1.8 miles north of the ranger station and follow signs to the trailhead at 5720ft.

Route

Follow the trail through often lovely woods about 3 miles to a junction on the SW slopes of the peak. Turn right and head up to the summit 0.6 miles on a primitive climber's trail. Remember where the trail stops at the lower edge of the summit talus field so you can find it on the descent.

Ladybugs in detail.

Crazy Peak (11,209ft — p 5,709ft)

Status
>Highpoint of the Crazy Mountains
>Prominence rank = 1
>Elevation rank = 55
>Sweetgrass County BP

Difficulty
>Day hike, partly on old road/trail
>7 miles RT with 4800ft gain
>Steep and rugged terrain, some scrambling, danger from loose rock

Other sources
>Websites: Summitpost
>Books: B-B, AIRG

Land status
>Gallatin NF & private

The Crazy Peak topo, along with several for Glacier National Park, is unique in having 80 foot contour lines. This is steep country! When you can find some solid rock, it's really a joy to climb. But there is much loose rock, which is both tiring and dangerous. So just slow down, be careful, and enjoy the stark beauty of these wild mountains.

Access to the Crazies is rather limited by the extensive private land holdings around and within the range. Fortunately, Crazy Peak is easily reached from the main east-side access. But note that the peak itself is on a section of private land, even though it's all 'rocks & ice' and not posted.

Driving

From US 191 about 11 miles north of Big Timber or 33 miles south of Harlowton, turn west onto Wormers Loop Rd, at a FS sign for Big Timber

(top) View up Big Timber Creek.
(bottom) Granite and Blue Lakes
below the north spur.

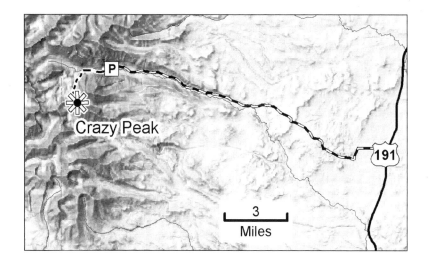

Canyon. It's then 16 miles to the end of the road at Halfmoon Campground ($5 per night in 2010) and the trailhead at 6450ft. The first 10 miles are fine, the last 6 are ruts and rocks, with a few potholes and a gate thrown in.

Route

The basic route is to gain the west ridge of the peak, follow it east to a false summit, then follow a climber's trail through a notch and around some gendarmes to the top—a section that involves some easy 3rd class scrambling.

The real work is reaching the west ridge, and the best way to do that depends on snow conditions and your comfort level with climbing on snow. When conditions and your skill level permit, a snow route is much preferred—safer, easier, and more fun—but note that too much snow can increase the difficulty and exposure of the scrambling section. Any one of several snow gullies on the north side of the west ridge will work, and these are best approached by hiking the trail up to Granite and Blue Lakes.

The route described below is an all-rock route and though not the easiest, it's the most direct and quite scenic.

Hike up the trail (actually an old access road for some mines on the slopes of Conical Mountain) to the second pack bridge over Big Timber Creek. Stay on the S side and bushwhack up and west to tree-line, then traverse west into the wide swale dropping from the summit. Aim for a ledgey ramp leading up to the spur ridge that defines the west edge of that swale, and follow that ramp up. Then pick your way up the occasionally narrow ridge straight to the false summit.. The best rock is usually right on the crest.

From the false summit, find a steep slot that drops straight down to a notch (3rd class). [NOTE: this notch is the head of the "Crazy Couloir"—a serious snow or ice climb from the east.] Then traverse, with some up & down, around the west side of a big pinnacle before heading up talus/scree to the top.

Crow Peak (9,415ft — p 3,775ft)

Status
> Highpoint of the Elkhorn Mountains
> Prominence rank = 23
> Jefferson County HP and BP

Difficulty
> Day hike (or snowshoe or ski), partly on old tracks/trail
> 8 miles RT with 3200ft gain
> Much talus or rubble in summer;
> baseless snow much of the winter (take rock skis!)

Other sources
> Websites: County Highpointers
> Books: HGM-79, CGM

Land status
> Beaverhead-Deerlodge NF

The Elkhorns are basically big piles of volcanic rubble that can be tedious walking. I generally climb here in winter and early spring, on snowshoes or skis. Fortunately, the road into the town of Elkhorn is plowed, providing easy access for day climbs of Crow Peak.

Driving:
It's about 12 miles of generally OK gravel road from MT 69 south of Boulder up to the town of Elkhorn. Drive through town to where the road levels out and swings sharply right. Park here at 6550ft.

Route:
Follow the road east about 100 yards to a "T", turn left (towards Iron Mine and Muskrat Creek trail) and go about 50 feet to a little-used track that veers gently up to the right. Follow this track up through pleasant but beetle-infested woods. It soon joins Elkhorn Creek and continues up along its east bank for a bit before slowly morphing to trail and then petering-out altogether at about 7600ft.

At this point you can either head east into and up the talus slope leading steeply but directly to the peak, or you can continue up the drainage, staying

Crow Peak from Elkhorn Peak.

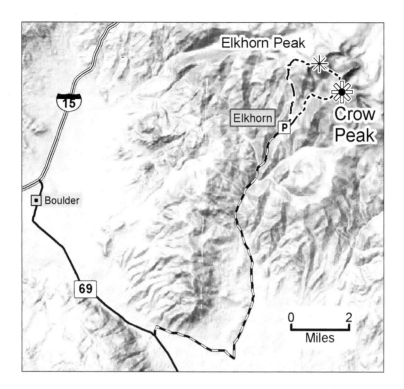

right at every fork, to the saddle due north of the summit. (If snow conditions are good, I ski or snowshoe the drainage; if not, I hike the slope.)

Since there's a chance that Elkhorn Peak is actually higher than Crow, you'd better loop over it before descending back to town. It means another 500 feet of elevation gain, but it's also the most scenic part of the hike, traversing above the cirques dropping to Tizer Basin and then past the marble cliffs on Elkhorn's southwest face.

From the top of Elkhorn Peak, drop steeply west to the saddle and continue west across the north side of Windy Point. When you hit the top of a steep talus slope, turn right and follow its upper edge down into the woods—heading NW into more open and dying forest (and possibly a new cabin and property boundary depending on your route) before dropping west again. Where the slope levels out, you should intersect the old Iron Mine road. Turn left and follow it down gently then steeply back to your vehicle.

Alternate route:

When snow conditions are really good, skin up the Iron Mine road to the flats then east up past the new cabin to Elkhorn Peak, traverse over to Crow, then descend Crow's east ridge to the saddle and drop due south to the road. Turn left and follow this road all the way down into Queen Gulch—a great run!—and then take the cut-off past the cemetery back to your vehicle.

Eighteenmile Peak (11,125ft — p 1,635ft)

Status

>Highest point on the Continental Divide in Idaho and Montana
>Elevation rank = 62

Difficulty

>Day hike on old and current vehicle routes, plus cross-country travel
>2.5–5 miles one-way with 2800ft to 3700ft gain
>(depending on where you park)
>Some steep scree and gentle talus on the top

Other sources

>Books: B-B, EIM

Land status

>Beaverhead-Deerlodge NF

This corner of Montana is truly "high, wide, and handsome", and the views from its higher summits are a peakbagger's delight *(see photos on page 126),* with beckoning peaks (albeit many in Idaho and some in Wyoming) in every direction. Like most of southwest Montana, early summer is the best time to visit, when the mountains still carry some snow and before the lower slopes get cowed-out. But this country is really lovely all year long.

Driving

The paved Westside Frontage Road runs between Dell (exit 23) and Lima (exit 15) along I-15. The Big Sheep Creek Road, a BLM Backcountry Byway, heads west from the frontage road about 2 miles south of Dell. Follow this scenic route for 18 miles, through 3 neat canyons, to a major fork and your first view of Eighteenmile Peak. The Byway goes right, you go left, then left again, following signs for Nicholia Creek.

About 23.5 miles from the frontage road stay left once more, then ford a ditch, drop to one or more fords of Cottonwood Creek by a cabin, and follow the now rutted dirt road to another fork just across the cattleguard marking the NF boundary. The first 100 yards of the right branch to Harkness Lakes is the worst—marginal for a 2WD vehicle. If you make it up the hill, where you park really depends on the hike you've planned. A good place for keeping your options open is 1.3 miles up where the road forks—right to the lakes, left to Bear Creek—at 7800ft.

Route

The best route up the mountain is to follow roads and old tracks up to the obvious NE ramp and climb that to the top. The country is totally open and mostly gentle, so you can pretty much take whatever route you want. There's a steep but good goat/climbers trail up the steep part of the ramp that angles left (S) to the divide. Then it's a short talus hop north to the summit.

From the summit, hard-core peakbaggers will want to traverse the divide north to bag COTTONWOOD (11,024ft—p 424ft). This option requires a bit of exposed scrambling getting off the summit, then about a mile of picky going along the ridge before you hit easier terrain. Once on top of

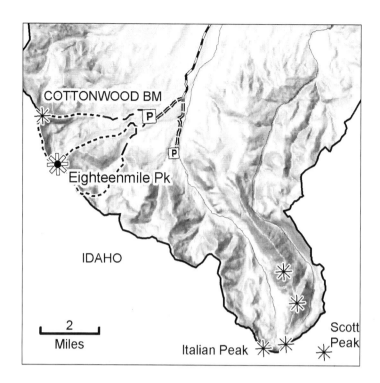

COTTONWOOD, drop down the east ridge and pick a route past Harkness Lakes to your vehicle.

The old, the infirm and the intelligent will prefer to loop south along the divide, a delightful ramble with a number of possible variations, one of which is described here. Follow the crest down to a prominent saddle, contour east around the ridge until you can drop down to a small, flat basin, cross the basin to the east edge of the lip and take a good game trail down to the saddle on the ridge that separates the two branches of Bear Creek. Follow that ridge up then down to the old track and on out to your vehicle.

Additional climbs

Having traveled this far into the SW corner of Montana, you really should spend more time here. I highly recommend a 2-night backpack into upper Nicholia Creek. There are delightful camps near some springs at about 9,000ft, below the pass going over to Deadman Creek. On the layover day, climb to the Divide via a couloir SE (left) of Italian Peak, then head SE to the southern-most point in Montana. Drop west and climb Scott Peak, skirting Pt 11,292 on the west. At 11,393 feet, it's the highpoint of the Beaverhead Mountains. Return to the ascent couloir and either drop to camp or tackle the airy 3rd class traverse across the two highpoints of Italian Peak, before descending a couloir further north down to the valley. For a several hour jaunt, hike to the pass and enjoy some spectacular views before climbing Peak 10,828 via the obvious ramp. Peaks 10,601 and 10,529 are also fun, and the former harbors an old airplane wreck on its south slope.

Electric Peak (10,992ft — p 3,412ft)

Status
　Highpoint of the Gallatin Range
　Elevation rank = 73
　Prominence rank = 35

Difficulty
　LONG day hike
　10 miles one way with 4000ft (SE ridge) or 6000ft (N ridge) gain
　Mix of old road, trail and cross-country travel
　This is grizzly country

Other sources
　Websites: Summitpost, County Highpointers
　Books: HYNP, SPGY

Land status
　Yellowstone NP, Gallatin NF (N ridge)

Electric Peak is huge, and an anomaly—it's over 500 feet higher than anything else in the range. It has two standard routes to the top, and both are wonderful hikes. There is a bit of exposure and scrambling on the top, especially on the SE ridge route, but nothing scary. Both routes are well-described in print and web sources. I like the easier north ridge route, described below, even though it involves more elevation gain and walking 5 miles (10 miles RT) on a road, because half of the distance is on a road and I don't get as beat up and worn out as I would after 20 miles of trail. And the road is really quite pleasant if you ignore the weeds.

Driving

From the Roosevelt Arch in Gardiner, go north about 4.5 miles to the Beattie Gulch TH, which is located just north of the Park boundary on the north side of Reese Creek at 5200ft. Or head south from the Corwin Springs bridge about 3.5 miles to the same spot.

Electric Peak from its north ridge.

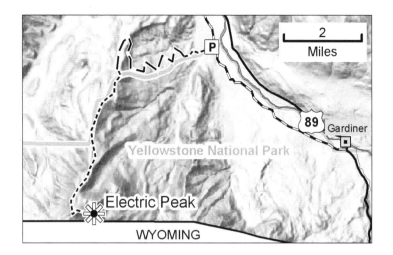

Route

A use trail heads west under the power lines to the first switchback in the road, and another continues west up the hill, cutting off the second switchback.

Then it's on up the road, onto private land (and FS easement), past some communications stuff at the ridge crest and around the cabins to the NF property boundary at the end of the road. The FS recently (2010) sawed out a route through the burn to the open ridge above. Head south over a blip to a NPS trail sign by the spring: "NE Electric Ridge—summit 4.8 miles". There may have been an actual trail at one time—but now it's a matter of following either game trails or little orange tabs or both (when they happen to coincide) up the ridge, over a wooded blip (Pt 9263) and into gorgeous open country.

Head up veg slopes to the shoulder on the west side of the west summit; then follow a climbers trail on broken rock right on the ridge crest—up over the west summit, down to the saddle and up to the higher east summit. On the return, if the snow is gone, you can use a game trail to cut across the NE face of the west summit.

South face and SE ridge of Electric Peak.

Elk Peak (8,566ft — p 2,766ft)

Status
> Highpoint of the Castle Mountains
> Prominence rank = 67

Difficulty
> Half-day hike on old road and trail
> 5 miles one-way with 1800ft gain
> short scramble on summit boulders

Other sources
> - none

Land status
> Lewis & Clark NF

The Castle Mountains are not really a 'range' in the usual sense, but rather a single big, gentle granitic blob. 'It' is mostly covered with pine forests, but with lots of pretty rock outcrops poking through. Elk Peak, the summit, is just the highest of these outcrops. (There is only one other p400 peak in the whole area, limy Whetstone Ridge located 10 miles to the east.)

The whole area is riddled with old mining roads, many of which are now ATV routes, plus a few user-created routes as well. So why include Elk Peak here? I like it: it's pretty, it's a unique landscape (when you get up on a rock outcrop and can see it!), and the walking is pleasant. Although the entire hike is on ATV routes, on a Sunday in July, I met just three. (Speaking as a "wildernut", it's nice to meet "motorheads" on their own turf: they're not defensive, I'm not angry, we can be civil towards one another.)

Driving

From MT 294 at about MP 15.5 turn north into bustle-free Lennep and then head west on the road to Castle Town. Drive through Castle Town (a sign in the midst of posted private property), and in a mile pass the NF sign. Timid drivers may park where the road levels out, bends right and narrows in a small saddle; but 2WD vehicles can continue another mile, going left shortly after, onto Road J15994 and then sharp left on the ridge top onto Road J8884, to park at an old mine building ("Yellowstone Mine") at 6950ft.

Route

Continue up the road, now an ATV route, about 1.5 miles, to where a road branches left up the hill and the ATVs have a well-worn track past the road closure. Take this branch—it's nicer walking than the main road and rejoins it at about 8000ft, at the start of a steep and loose section that leads up to the crest. Follow the route up and down along the crest, being sure to clamber up "Elk Peak #1—Wapiti Peak", before passing three signed junctions as you curve around and head for "Elk Peak #2—Elk Peak". There's a small repeater station nestled in the summit, but it doesn't ruin the view.

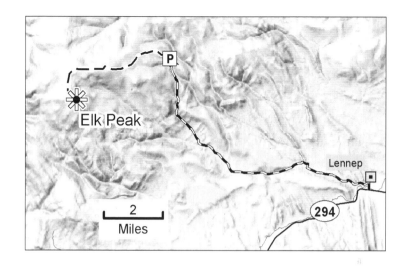

ATV track heading towards the summit of Elk Peak.

Garfield Mountain (10,961ft — p 3,281ft)

Status

Highpoint of the Lima Peaks subrange of the Beaverhead Mountains
Elevation rank = 74
Prominence rank = 39

Difficulty

In & out or loop day hike, mostly cross-country
9–10 miles RT with 4,000ft to 5,000ft of gain
Mostly a grassy walk, with some talus on top.

Other sources

Website: Summitpost

Land status

Beaverhead-Deerlodge NF

I pretty much detest quartzite. It's very hard and often fairly smooth, which makes quartzite rubble and talus unstable, and that makes for tedious and tiresome walking. But it is often a very pretty rock, and some of the quartzite in the Lima Peaks is jaw-dropping gorgeous. The rock in turn imbues the mountains' slopes with varied, subtle hues. Add in the veg and trees and, my gosh, this is beautiful country!

Driving

From Lima (exit 15 on I15) take the Westside Frontage Road about 1/2 mile NW to the Little Sheep Creek Road, turn left (west) and follow signs for East Creek Campground, about 8.5 miles from the highway, at 7,000ft.

Garfield Mountain from the northwest.

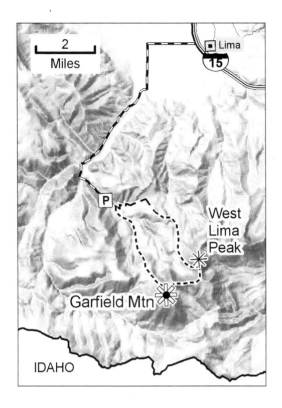

Route

Because of all the small and slightly unstable talus on these mountains, it's best to stay on the veg as much as possible. The NW ridge route does that and is quite direct.

If you don't want to camp or park in the shade, turn left across the creek about 1/3 mile before the campground then stay right at a fork and park by the old car body. If you park in the campground, cross the creek and walk up the road 10 minutes to this same spot. Continue up the track to its end at the creek. Cross the creek and follow an old ATV track through tall grass and lovely aspens about 1/4 mile to the sharp ridge on the east side of a prominent drainage. Head up this ridge and aim for the steep, talus-capped knoll ahead. Avoid the talus by traversing left and then follow the grassy slope to the base of the peak. With foresight you can stay mostly on veg all the way to the saddle north of the peak. Then head south up the ridge to the huge cairn marking the summit. (The bench mark is about 40 feet south and 2 feet lower.)

The traverse over to West Lima Peak is definitely worth doing—the talus is mostly fun, the route is obviously scenic, some of the rocks on West Lima are gorgeous, and the descent route via the ridge and track marking the east and north side of the East Fork drainage, over Pt 8245, is gentle and lovely. From the top of West Lima it's best to backtrack south to the saddle, drop west to the bench (a huge flophouse for elk) and loop around back to its NW ridge—the direct descent is steep and loose.

Glacier National Park mountains

Kintla Peak (10,101ft — p 4,401ft)
Highpoint of the Livingston Range
Flathead County BP
Prominence rank = 8

Mount Cleveland (10,466ft — p 5,226ft)
Highpoint of the Lewis Range
Glacier County HP & BP
Prominence rank = 4

Mount Stimson (10,142ft — p 4,382ft)
Flathead County HP
Southern Lewis Range HP
Prominence rank = 9

These are the toughest peaks in this guide. I'm lumping them together for several reasons: they are all in Glacier, so climbers have to abide by the Park's backcountry regulations; they are all in serious grizzly country, so climbing parties of 4 or more are recommended; they all require multi-day backpack trips (for mere mortals anyway—they've all been done as day hikes!); and their climbs require good route-finding plus some luck to avoid excessive exposure.

In addition, I've climbed them all just once, back in the early 1990s when I didn't record much detail about my climbs. So these accounts of necessity will be sketchy and anecdotal. All three peaks are covered in Edward's *Climber's Guide to Glacier National Park*, and all three have pages on *Summitpost*.

Kintla Peak
This was a long day from the Boulder Pass campsite. We traversed around the basin, with considerable up & down, crossed the outflow from Agassiz Glacier, then ascended the east spur and junk-rock gullies to the top. The most difficult part was the creek crossing—especially on the return when the warm day had increased flows—and a steep couloir getting onto the east spur. The overall trip was an in & out from Goat Haunt, taking two days each way to & from Boulder Pass.

Mount Cleveland
This climb was a long day from the Stony Indian Lake campsite. The worst part was climbing and traversing the scree to the notch south of the main Stony Indian Peaks. The ledges on the east side were fine, except we had to belay across one snow-filled couloir, and the south ridge up to the top is just a walk. This trip was an A to B from Goat Haunt to Chief Mountain border station, with a key-exchange at Mokowanis Lake.

Kinnerly Peak looming above the start of the climb up Kintla. (B.Bucher photo)

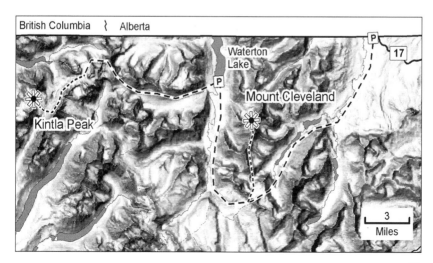

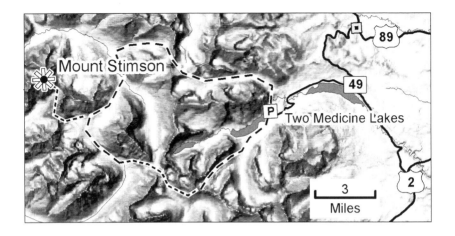

Mount Stimson

And yet another long day from a camp at Buffalo Woman Lake (a better base but worse camp than Beaver Woman). We climbed to the saddle south of Pinchot and traversed its west face on scree and ledges to the south ridge of Stimson, then steep scree with short, easy steps up to the top. Parts of the traverse can be quite exposed, depending on your luck in picking a ledge system to follow.

Our approach to Stimson was different and quite nice. From Two Medicine, hike the trail southwest to the Continental Divide, then traverse mostly open slopes around Mount Rockwell to a lovely camp at Aurice Lake. A somewhat tricky traverse leads into the next basin, then easy going leads to and through the notch between Caper Peak and Lone Walker Mountain, and down to the broad saddle SE of Mount Phillips. From here we traversed NW on game trails just below the cliffs into an open gully and followed it down to the Coal Creek trail and on up to Buffalo Woman Lake. (This whole area was toasted in the 2003 Rampage fire, so some other route may be better.) After the climb we hiked out to Two Med via Surprise Pass and Pitamakan Pass.

Stoney Indian traverse. (B.Bucher photo)

(left) South face of Mount Stimson from the traverse on Mount Pinchot. (B.Bucher photo)(right) Climbing the south face of Mount Stimson. (B.Bucher photo)

Granite Peak (12,799ft — p 4,759ft)

Status
> Highest Point in Montana and the Beartooth Mountains
> Prominence rank = 5
> Park County HP & BP

Difficulty
> Multi-day backpack via FS trail, climbers trail and cross-country
> Summit requires moderately exposed 3rd class climbing;
> steep snow (icy in the morning) is likely through July

Other sources
> Websites: Summitpost, County Highpointers, Custer NF
> Books: HGM79&94, SPGY, CGM, HM04, AIRG

Land status
> Custer NF, Absaroka-Beartooth Wilderness

Granite Peak may be the most difficult and the most popular peak in the Beartooths. Because it is covered so well in other print and web sources, I limit the material here to personal comments.

There are two 'easy' routes on the mountain: the east ridge and the southwest couloir. I have not done the SW couloir; I've climbed the east ridge 3 times. Once we didn't use the rope at all; once I belayed Sara down a section, and once I belayed a different section both up & down. If you find the easiest route, it's only 3rd class. But you might not find it, in which case it can be quite a bit harder. Always bring a rope.

There are three approaches to the east ridge. Froze-to-Death Plateau from the Mystic Lake TH may be the most popular. Use it later in the season, when the plateau is less squishy and when you won't have icy snow on the climbers trail down to the saddle in the morning. Tempest Mountain (12,469ft) is easy pickings from here.

Huckleberry Creek is also popular. It's best earlier in the season, when snow covers the ice and debris of the Granite Glacier and affords a fine glissade on the descent. Camp in or near the saddle above Avalanche Lake and leave the big talus on the east side of the lake for summit day. This is also the best spot from which to bag Mystic Mountain (12,080+ft).

Granite Peak and Tempest Mountain, with Mount Wood in the background.

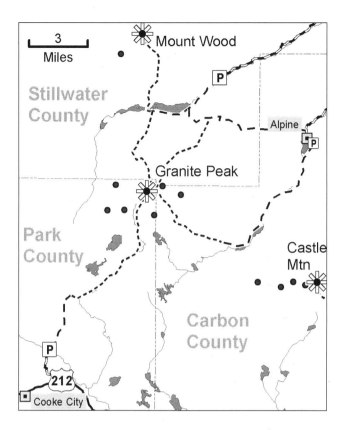

The 'best' approach is from the south. Hike up the East Rosebud trail from Alpine to the bridge over Granite Creek, then bushwhack up the creek past Echo Lake and the tarn above it onto the ridge to the north. Pick a route (veg & some talus) up the ridge then N to a base camp between Granite and Lowary Lakes. This approach requires two days; but the East Rosebud is the most spectacular drainage & trail in the range and worth the hike on its own. This base camp also works for the SW couloir route.

The standard approach for the SW couloir is up Sky Top Creek from the Fisher Creek TH northeast of Cooke City. A good trail, mostly sawed out and well cairned, branches east after crossing the Broadwater River and leads up to Lone Elk Lake. The uppermost parts of the drainage, below the SW face, present much scree and morainal material, and the couloir is reportedly icy in places, especially once the snow has melted off.

A camp above the inlet to Rough Lake also works as a base for climbs of Glacier Peak (12,351ft) and Mount Villard (12,345ft), both accessed via an easy, low pass to Upper Aero Lake, plus Cairn Mountain (12,220ft) by its lovely south ridge, and two delightful 'warm-up' climbs: Peak 11,379 and Peak 10,952. Note: this is bear country, so bring a bear-proof canister for your food.

Great Northern Mountain
(8,705ft — p 2,505ft)

Status
> Highpoint of the Flathead Range
> Prominence rank = 85

Difficulty
> Day hike on climber's trail
> 4 miles one-way with 4900ft gain
> Steep in places, some exposure

Other sources
> Websites: Summitpost
> Books: HGM79&94, HM04, CGM

Land status
> Flathead NF

The Flathead Range is really just a subrange of the Lewis & Clark Range. It has been singled out, and its highest point named, because of its location above the Middle Fork Flathead River and the Great Northern Railway line. But both features, the range and the peak, deserve their notoriety. The climb of Great Northern is a thrilling hike in a spectacular location, with ever larger views of Glacier NP and the Hungry Horse-Swan Range country unfolding as you gain elevation. It is also ideal for hikers who are new to peakbagging—the route is trail all the way, but *climber's* trail—often steep, occasionally rough, occasionally braided, and exposed in a couple of spots.

Driving

Turn east off US 2 into Martin City, veer right onto Central Ave and head up the east side of Hungry Horse Reservoir. The pavement ends in two miles; the gravel road is excellent but often busy and dusty. About 16 miles from US 2 you reach a junction with roads branching to the right and left. The right-right branch climbs steeply up to Firefighter Mountain and a lookout tower with a great view of Great Northern. You want the left branch, which heads NE and ends in 0.6 miles after crossing Hungry Horse Creek at 4250ft.

Route

The well-trodden trail starts at the parking spot on the north side of the creek and climbs steeply NE up a spur ridge for 2400ft (in about one mile) to the gentle and open main ridge. Having paid your dues, the rest is pure joy: just follow the trail, with some ups and downs (this is Belt formation country), as it slowly arcs around to the summit. When you get past the last trees (and the most exposed section of the hike) the trail will often braid into two or more tracks. Stay on or nearest the crest of the ridge for the best route: it's not as loose there, and the scenery is better. The obvious cliff band that cuts the ridge a bit north of the summit can be dicey if there is snow (bring an ice axe) or the ground is wet—otherwise it's just hiking. And once on top, give thanks that the eastern summit is lower!

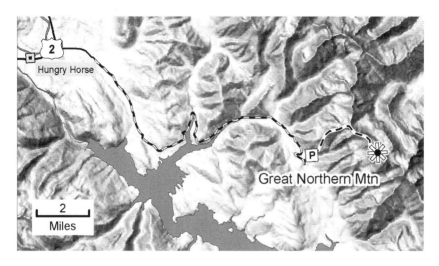

(above) NW ridge of
Great Northern Mtn.
(left) Nearing the
summit of Great
Northern Mtn.

Haystack Mountain (8,821+ft — p 2,381+ft)

Status
Highpoint of the Boulder Mountains
Prominence rank = 96
Difficulty
Half-day hike on National Recreation Trail
3-4 miles one-way with 2200-2600ft gain
Other sources
- none
Land status
Beaverhead-Deerlodge NF

Haystack is basically a pleasant but non-descript blob of a mountain—except for the summit and last 1/2 mile of trail, which is very scenic and affords great views. The trailhead is easy to find and the trail is in good shape—a perfect hike for beginning peakbaggers.

Most maps show its elevation as 8819ft (8821ft according to the NGS) , but the bench mark is a clear 8-10' lower than the summit (it was placed when the lookout covered the summit).

Summit boulders on Haystack Mountain.

Driving

From exit 138 off I-15 in Elk Park, take the east-side frontage road north for 4.8 miles, turn right onto gravel Haystack Road, and continue 0.7 miles to a gate. Either park here at 6200ft or continue up the occasionally rutted road a long mile to road's end at the trailhead at 6650ft.

Route

Hike up the trail in pine-beetle infested woods, crossing several small creeks, to the old lookout site. The scenery and views improve the higher you get. At least 20 different mountain ranges are visible from the top.

Highwood Baldy (7,670ft — p 3,290ft)

Status
> Highpoint of the Highwood Mountains
> Chouteau County HP & BP
> Prominence rank = 38

Difficulty
> Short day hike on old trail and cross-country
> 3.5 miles one-way with 3300ft gain
> Some gnarly krumholz and loose talus up high

Other sources
> Websites: Summitpost, County Highpointers
> Books: HGM79&94

Land status
> Lewis & Clark NF

The Highwoods are just gorgeous in spring. Unfortunately, Highwood Baldy, with its road, communications junk and loose talus on top is not the nicest destination. But it is the HP. So I present a perfunctory description of the most aesthetic ascent route and then describe a truly wonderful hike—a loop over the 2nd & 4th highest peaks in the range. (Note: the 1995 topo maps show the trails all wrong; the Forest Visitors map shows them right.)

Driving

The Highwood Creek Road leaves MT 228 about 6 miles north of its junction with MT 331 and heads SE & E up the drainage for 12.5 miles to the NF boundary and

Highwood Baldy from the east.

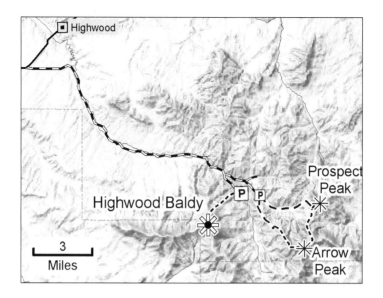

a fork. For Highwood Baldy, take the right fork a short mile through two fords to the Deer Creek TH at 4400ft. For Prospect & Arrow Peaks, stay left for a long mile to a second fork, then right 1/2 mile to the TH at road's end at 4550ft.

Route

The trail up along the SE side of Deer Creek is lovely but short: it ends in a couple of miles at about 5500 feet. Climb W up to the ridge (you can also just follow this ridge from the crossing of Highwood Creek at the TH) and continue up open slopes on the broad north ridge of the peak. Follow the meadowy ground, slightly east of the crest, to its highest point, then angle up west through gnarly woods until you break out on talus slopes and can mostly follow these to the top.

Prospect Peak (6,549ft — p 650ft)
Arrow Peak (7,485ft — p 1930ft)

From the North Fork TH, hike up the trail about 4.5 miles, past three signed junctions, to the pass SW of Prospect Peak at 5900ft. Climb Prospect via its mostly open SW ridge and return to the pass. Follow the divide south on game trails and open slopes to Point 6746 and down to the saddle at the base of Arrow Peak. The 1000 feet up to the top can be gnarly (dog-hair, talus), especially if snow drifts restrict your options. After enjoying the wonderful views, drop NW, dogleg west to Point 6890, then head NW again down the ridge until you cut trail # 415. Turn left and follow this incredibly scenic trail: it drops through a drainage then climbs back to and follows the ridge between Highwood Creek and its North Fork before dropping east to the TH and your vehicle.

Hilgard Peak (11,297ft — p 4,044ft)

Status
> Highpoint of the Madison Range
> Madison County HP & BP
> Elevation rank = 48
> Prominence rank = 15

Difficulty
> Day hike partly on trail with 3rd class scramble on summit
> 7.5 miles one-way with 5,500ft gain
> A long day but not psychologically demanding

Other sources
> Websites: Summitpost, County Highpointers
> Books: SPGY, CGM

Land status
> Beaverhead-Deerlodge & Gallatin NF
> Lee Metcalf Wilderness

The second-highest range in the state has many notable peaks, all of which are worthy objectives for a peakbagger. Gallatin Peak dominates the northern, Spanish Peaks section. It is most easily climbed via a veg-rock couloir on its west face, from a camp at or above Thompson Lake—a full-day's pack from any of three east-side trailheads.

Views of, and access to, the rest of the range are better from the broad, open Madison Valley on the west. Sphinx and Cedar Mountains are best climbed from the Bear Creek TH, as is Lone Mountain, via its SW ridge from a camp in Muddy Creek—a much longer but very much nicer route than dealing with Big Sky.

The major peaks in the southern part of the range, Koch, Imp, Echo and Hilgard, are not as visually prominent as those in the north. But the country south of Indian and Shedhorn Creeks is wilder and more rugged, and Hilgard Peak (with the possible exception of Beehive) is the most difficult climb in the range.

Hilgard Peak and its east ridge, from the south.

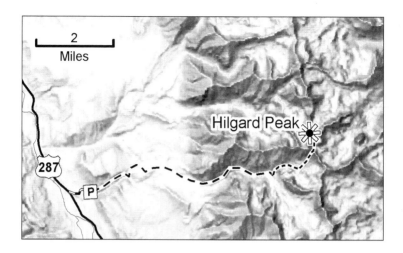

Driving

The Papoose Creek access takes off east from US 287 a bit south of the West Fork Rest Area, at about MP 15.5. Head up the hill 0.6 miles to the huge, shade-less parking area at 6,100ft.

Route

Follow the trail (an old road) through a bit of private land and then up to a bench and a trail junction. Stay right and continue another gentle mile past potential campsites and into the canyon. Where the trail bends right (south) to follow the main drainage, leave it and bushwhack up along the north branch of the creek—steep but OK game trails pass the cascade on its north side. Head east into the basin, past a lovely campsite where the creek forks, to the base of the talus slopes dropping from Pt 11,061. Climb steeply up to the obvious smooth little saddle on its SE ridge and drop 200 feet on gentle snow into the basin below Hilgard's SE face. Head north to the saddle on its east ridge and then scramble to the top. The summit is on the north side of the east ridge; but you can climb the easier south side and then traverse north around the ridge higher up or even along the crest. This is solid 3rd class scrambling with some exposure—but if you remember to zig before you zag, it's not as hard as it looks.

Second-highest **Koch Peak (11,293ft – p 1,193ft)** is usually climbed as a day hike from the east, via the road up Taylor Fork. Although it requires a camp up Shedhorn Creek, I prefer the approach from the west for several reasons: the road to the Indian Creek TH is much better than the Taylor Fork road; Shedhorn Creek is itself a delight—full of lovely meadows and wildlife; and a multi-day trip permits climbs of other fun peaks in the area, like Peak 10,829, Peak 10,705, Peak 10,764 and Shedhorn Peak.

Holland Peak (9,356ft — p 3,996ft)

Status
>   Highpoint of the Swan Range
>   Prominence rank = 16 or 17
>   possibly Missoula County BP (tied with Ch-paa-qn Peak)

Difficulty
>   Day hike on good climbers trail
>   4 miles one-way with 5200ft gain
>   Some steep and brushy ground, borderline scrambling

Other sources
>   Websites: Summitpost
>   Books: CGM

Land status
>   Flathead NF
>   on Bob Marshall Wilderness boundary

The Swan Range stretches for almost 100 miles, from Bad Rock Canyon on the Flathead River south to — well, its southern boundary is not really clear, but I put it at Monture Creek and the Blackfoot River. Its steep west face looms over the Clearwater and Swan Valleys the whole way and is capped by many fine peaks, especially between rugged Swan Peak in the north and Fisher Peak in the south. Holland Peak lies in the middle of this stretch, and its easy access, spectacular route and fine views make it a very popular climb.

Driving

From MT 83 a few miles south of Condon, follow FS Road # 560 (Rumble Creek Road) east to the Cooney Lookout and park at the TH a bit beyond (3.5 miles from the highway) at 4550ft.

Route

Hike the trail a short mile to about 100 yards past the crossing of the north fork of Rumble Creek. Look for a well-beaten track heading up along the north edge of a brush field. Follow this trail, occasionally quite steeply, up and up and up—then over to the creek and up some more to the lower lake. Go around the south shore and continue up on occasionally steep and rough trail, with some scree & talus, to the spectacular upper lake nestled beneath the peak's western cliffs. From the outlet, the trail continues south up a steep veg-rock face and then peters-out on the gentle ridge below Point 8852. There's a neat slabby stretch in the saddle north of Pt 8852, where you might want an ice axe early in the season; then it's scree and ledges to the top.

For solitude and adventure, consider a backpack trip to the lake basins southeast of the peak. The climb from Holland Lake up to the old lookout site on Point 8053 is a real grunt, and the traverse north past the Necklace Lakes to Rubble Lake or the Terrace Lakes can be tiresome. But you'll have some gorgeous,

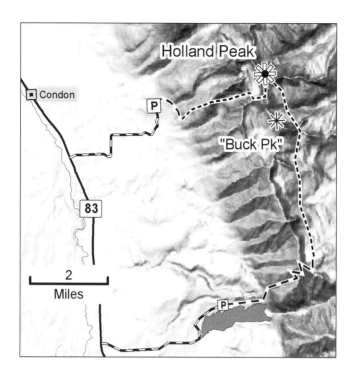

wild country all to yourself. To climb Holland, cross through the double notch at 7600ft north of Terrace Lakes, traverse over to the SE face and head up scree and easy steps to the top. To return, follow the divide south over Peak 9003 ("Buck Peak")—a few spots approach 3rd class, but it's mostly easy, pleasant going.

Swan Peak (9,289 ft – p 2289 ft)

Second-highest Swan Peak is even more spectacular than Holland Peak. Like Holland, there is a climber's trail that provides a direct route from the west (do a web search for Swan Peak Montana) and a longer route via FS trail up Lion Creek to the south and east. The "climber's route" is fun but demanding. I'd suggest packing a camp about 8 miles up the wild and scenic Lion Creek trail, then bushwhacking up the drainage (somewhat gnarly), following the obvious ramp to the saddle, and walking the easy but breathtaking east ridge to the top.

Hollowtop Mountain (10,604ft — p 3,884ft)

Status
>Highpoint of the Tobacco Root Mountains
>Prominence rank = 20

Difficulty
>Day hike, partly on old road/ATV route
>2.5 miles one-way with 3700ft gain
>Steep ground, with an option for a bit of easy scrambling

Other sources
>Books: B-B

Land Status
>Beaverhead-Deerlodge NF

The Roots, like most mineral-rich ranges, have lots of old roads and tracks and, unfortunately, lots of ORV use. They are also pretty badly cowed-out by late summer. But they are still very scenic and lots of fun to hike around in, and the terrain is perfect for beginning peakbaggers: steep and with an alpine feel, but never too hard or gnarly.

Meadow along trail to Hollowtop Lake.

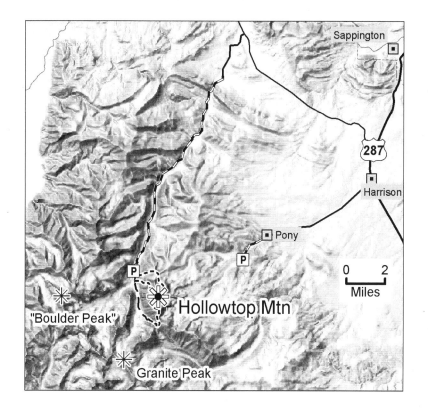

The highpoint, Hollowtop Mountain, can be approached from either the east, via Pony, or the west via the South Boulder River road. The shortest approach is from Pony via the now-closed track to Minor Lake, but getting to that road closure requires a 4WD vehicle. Although the trail to Hollowtop Lake is delightful, routes up the mountain from there are pretty gnarly. So I try to just relax and enjoy the long drive up the South Boulder in order to climb the steep but scenic and pleasant west face. The South Boulder also provides access to second-highest Granite Peak (10,590), which offers the best view in the range, and third-highest "Peak 10,574".

Driving

From MT 359 about 5 miles south of Cardwell, turn south onto the South Boulder Road. Follow this road up the scenic valley for about 15 miles, through the community of Mammoth, to a large meadow where the valley forks. Park by the outhouse and FS info sign at 6900ft.

Route

NOTE: you'll need footwear that can hold an edge in steep duff and veg; sneakers won't work on this route!

Walk up the old road/ATV route, signed "East Fork Trail". Cross the river on a bridge immediately below the forks and continue upstream 1/4 mile to a meadow at the base of an obvious cleft in the canyon wall. The route goes up the meadow, then follows game trails up 3rd class duff along the north side of the cascade onto a gentler, rockier little ridge. The drainage splits (and the creek goes underground) about this elevation. You need to get into the southern branch; so at the first glimpse of talus slopes above, traverse to the right and up through woods, aiming for the base of the major ridge to the south. Once in the open go up veggie gravel in the bottom and follow the drainage as it curves south and opens into a steep but lovely veg slope. (OR, head due east to the pass and climb Hollowtop's north ridge.) Exit the drainage to the west, aiming for a point a bit above the last trees on the ridge (ca. 9500ft), then enjoy the flowers and views as you wander up the ridge and plateau to the top.

There are several other west-face routes, if you care to make a loop with your descent. One follows the main crest south over Mt Jefferson and Horse Mountain, a scenic and pleasant walk, before dropping to the saddle and road to Nicholson Mine. Go north towards the mine a bit, then drop to the ATV route that leads back, albeit with several steep and unpleasantly loose sections, to the trailhead.

Another drops north into the 'hollow' and down its east edge to the pretty basin and tarn at 8800ft, then heads north across the crest at about 9100 and loops west into an obvious drainage that drops you between the bridge and trailhead.

Other peaks

Granite Peak is more easily approached via the old mining roads in South Willow Creek out of Pony or from the trail to Rossiter 'Lake' up Indian Creek out of Sheridan. But the climb from the South Boulder is lovely, and mostly pleasant if you can find the old FS trail on the west side of the East Fork. Try walking up the ATV route to the next big meadow past the takeoff for Hollowtop and then cross to the west side of the drainage and look for the trail. Once and if you find it, the old trail goes up to and disappears at a huge swampy meadow. Continue south around the meadow and into the lovely upper basin, then up the NW slopes of the peak. (About 5 miles one-way with 3700ft gain.)

For "Peak 10,574" (Pk N of Lakeshore Mtn), drive back down the road 1/2 mile to the lower Curly Lake TH. Hike up to the lake and continue past the junction with the upper trail to where the trail switchbacks and starts heading towards "Peak 10,059" (which is another lovely hike!). Leave the trail at the switchback and head SW (faint old trail to cabin, occasional blazes) up to a meadowy bench at 9800ft. From here follow the obvious ridge S to Pt 10,426 and then SW to the peak, often on good goat trail. (About 5 miles one-way, 3.5 of it on trail, with 4000ft gain.)

View of Granite Peak, from Hollowtop, Tobacco Root Mountains.

Homer Youngs Peak (10,621ft — p 3,201ft)

Status
> Highpoint of the 'West Big Hole' subrange of the Beaverhead Mountains
> Prominence rank = 43

Difficulty
> In & out day hike, or loop with some scrambling, mostly on trail
> 13 to 16 miles RT with 3200ft to 3400ft gain depending on where you park
> Lots of boggy sections on the trails, lots of talus on the peak
> Some easy but exposed scrambling on the west ridge

Other sources
> - none

Land status
> Beaverhead-Deerlodge NF

The SW ridge of this peak is a good introduction to exposure and scrambling—neither is very bad, and you can take the easy SE ridge down. The rock is highly fractured, which makes it easier to climb but also easier to break loose and fall. Be careful about where you step and what you hang onto.

Driving

About 1/2 mile south of Jackson the Miners Lake Road heads west from MT 278 for 10.6 rocky rough miles to a trailhead a bit past the campground loop at Lower Miners Lake. From here the road is passable to 2WD vehicles, but very rough and slow. It's 1.4 miles to the Kelly Creek trail and another 1.2 miles to the end of driving at the CDT trailhead. Both are at 7200ft.

If you just want to go in & out on the Kelly Creek trail, look for an old track heading up the hill just before the road starts descending gently back towards the creek.

Route

This loop can be done either direction. The southwest ridge (approached via the CDT to Rock Island Lakes) is fairly steep while the southeast ridge (approached via the Kelly Creek trail) is gentler. This description goes clockwise—up the

SE ridge of Homer Youngs Peak.

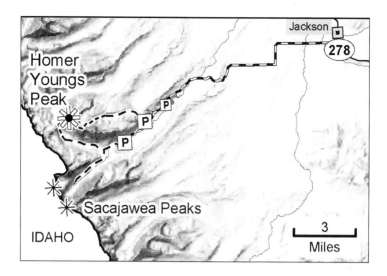

SW ridge and down the SE.

From the CDT trailhead, follow the old track/CDT up to lower Rock Island Lake, then continue on the trail past the outlet of the upper lake to where the CDT starts climbing out of the basin. Bushwhack north to and along the west shore of the upper lake and up to the saddle and the base of the SW ridge, then follow the ridge to the top. Except for avoiding the krumholz, it's best to stay on the ridge crest—the rock is better (still highly fractured but fairly stable).

From the summit, descend the SE ridge to the flat blip (Pt 9966ft) where it turns east, then descend the ridge heading NE to the first saddle and drop east (right) to a lovely gentle basin. In order to pick up the end of the Kelly Creek trail, continue NE along the base of the ridge you just descended, dropping into and down a small drainage until you hit an old lake, now a swamp. Look for a cairn at the edge of the meadow SE of the lake, marking the end (start for you) of the trail.

At the signed junction by the ditch, cross the ditch and follow the trail on down to the road. It goes straight across a small bog at one point before dropping steeply to the old track and road.

Other peaks

Homer Youngs Peak is a lovely mountain with a spectacular view, but the neatest spot in the whole range is actually the Upper Miner Lakes basin. If you've driven in as far as the Kelly Creek TH, by all means continue to the CDT TH and spend another day hiking up to those lakes, and climbing Monument Peak (10,323ft) and the highest Sacajawea Peak to the south (10,390ft). From the trail's end at the lake (good camping), climb SW up veg & rock onto a prominent ledge system with a good goat trail (and some exposure) that leads up to the ridge (Continental Divide) between the two peaks. From there, easy rock-hopping leads to either summit.

McDonald Peak (9,820ft — p 5,640ft)

Status
>Highpoint of the Mission Range
>Lake County HP & BP
>Prominence rank = 2

Difficulty
>A major undertaking from any direction.
>Backpack 4 miles on trail with 900ft gain, then
>Day hike about 3 miles one-way with 5500ft gain
>Bring ice-axe early in the season
>[Note: The peak and its slopes are closed to all entry from July 15–Oct. 1]

Other sources
>Websites: Summitpost, County Highpointers
>Books: HGM79, CGM

Land status
>CSKT-tribal land & Mission Mountains Tribal Wilderness
>Lolo NF & Mission Mountains Wilderness

McDonald is most often climbed by its south slope, which can be accessed either from Ashley Creek on the west or from Island Lake on the east. The route described here goes up the tributary to Post Creek that drains the north face of the peak; you bushwhack up to the basin below McDonald Glacier, go up the basin and climb to McDonald's NW ridge, and follow the ridge to the top.

Driving

First, if you're not a CSKT member, get a permit to recreate on Indian lands. Don't forget a camping stamp if you plan to camp on the reservation.

From US 93 between St. Ignatius and Ronan, head east on McDonald Lake Road to a 'T' just across a canal, turn left for the lake, cross the dam and turn right and park at the end of the road, about 5.5 miles from the highway, at 3600ft.

Route

McDonald Peak from near the divide above Island Lake.

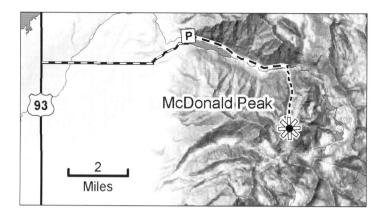

Hike up the scenic trail about 4 miles, with intimidating views of the peak looming above, to where the trail drops into a beautiful cedar grove with level, open camping sites along the creek. Cross Post Creek on a log and angle west (right) as you head up through the woods. You need to be near the east side of the tributary creek, to find the easiest passage through the several cliff bands that cross the slope.

Depending on water levels, you may encounter some 3rd class rock. You will invariably encounter 3rd class brush—bring good gloves for the hand-over-hand sections. The route is somewhat desperate up to about 5700ft, then just steep up to the rim of the basin at 6900ft. From here on the climb is a delight—you still have 3000 feet to go, but the walking is mostly pleasant and the scenery is inspirational. Just pick a line up the west side of the basin to the ridge and head on up.

McDonald Peak from McDonald Lake.

McGuire Mountain (6,991ft — p 3,071ft)

Status
> Highpoint of the Salish Mountains
> Prominence rank = 47

Difficulty
> Half-day hike on trail
> 3 miles one-way with 1600ft gain

Other sources
> - none

Land status
> Kootenai NF

McGuire involves a bunch of driving for a pretty short hike. But the last half mile is so gorgeous, the old lookout is so quaint (it's for rent if you want to spend the night) and the clearcuts are so photogenic that you won't mind the long drive. This peak is easily incorporated into a multi-day trip through the Yaak region, as briefly described under Northwest Peak.

Old lookout on McGuire Mountain.

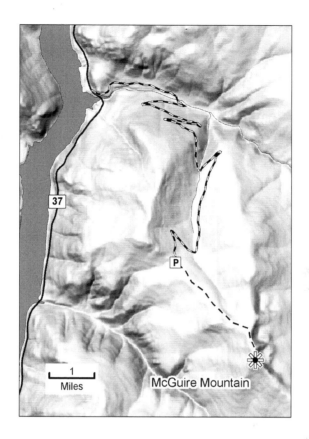

Driving

From MT 37 about 5 miles south of the Lake Koocanusa bridge, head east up the Sutton Creek Road for 2 miles, then another 10 miles up the Flat Creek Road to the TH in a saddle at 5450ft.

Route

The trail climbs SE up a gentle ridge, first in decadent lodgepole pine woods and along the edge of 1980s era clearcuts, then in ever more scenic woods until breaking out on the lovely open slopes below the lookout.

McLeod Peak (8,620ft — p 3,740ft)

Status
    Highpoint of the Rattlesnake Mountains
    Prominence rank = 25

Difficulty
    Day hike, partly on trail
    5 miles one-way with 4400ft gain
    More challenging and strenuous than the numbers suggest

Other sources
    Books: CGM
    Website: Rocky Mountaineers

Land status
    CSKT tribal land
    Lolo NF & Rattlesnake Wilderness

McLeod Peak is a spectacular viewpoint. It is commonly approached from the FS side—up the Rattlesnake drainage and then cross-country from the old road or trail in the uppermost reaches of the creek. But the route up the East Fork of Finley Creek is a scenic, varied and fun ramble through pretty and wild country, and it avoids the long hike or bike up the Rattlesnake road.

Driving

First, if you're not a CSKT member, get a permit to recreate on Indian lands.

From US 93 between Evaro and Arlee, head east on McClure Road for 0.8 miles and turn right (S) on a road by several mailboxes. Follow this road past several houses and onto 'Indian Land'. At 0.4 miles from McClure Road, cross a ditch and take the right branch. This dirt logging track is variously rutted, rocky and steep, but with care a 2WD vehicle can drive another 2 miles to its end in a small, slopey clearing at 4600ft.

View north of Missions and Swans from McLeod Peak.

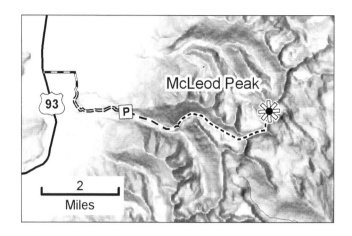

Route

Head up the infrequently maintained but well-used and scenic trail as it weaves its way, up, down, and around, along the north side of the creek. Follow it up through an open talus slope to where it starts to head down towards a crossing of the north branch of the creek. Leave the trail and continue up on a climbers trail through the talus and into the north branch drainage. Bushwhack up this drainage to the basin at its head, staying on the north side up out of the gnarly bottom, looking for that sweet spot along the base of the talus. Pick a route east to NE up to the ridge and follow it around (and up & down—this is Belt formation country) to the top.

McLeod Peak from where one hits the main divide.

Mount Cowen (11,212ft — p 2,652ft)

Status
> Highpoint of the Montana portion of the Absaroka Range
> Elevation rank = 54
> Prominence rank = 73

Difficulty
> Two or 3 day backpack with camp at Elbow Lake
> Backpack is 7.5 miles one-way with 3700ft gain in, 700ft gain out
> Climb is 1.5 miles one-way with 2600ft gain
> about half veg and half talus &/or snow
> exposed 3rd class scramble required

Other sources
> Websites: Summitpost
> Books: HGM79, SPGY, CGM

Land status
> Gallatin NF, Absaroka-Beartooth Wilderness

This popular peak deserves its popularity—the whole area is awesome the way we expect mountains to be. Even if you're not up for the exposed summit, it's worth the trek as far as you're comfortable, just to experience the place.

Cowen has three ridges (W, S, NE) and three faces (SW, E, N). The scrambler's route goes up to the W ridge, traverses onto and zig-zags up the SW face, hits the S ridge about 50ft below the summit, and climbs that to a broad ledge on the E face. Getting this far requires mostly walking with occasional climbing moves and minimal exposure—and you're just 20ft below the summit!

Driving
From US 89 south of Livingston turn south onto paved Mill Creek Road and follow it into the canyon. About 3+ miles up the gravel road, turn left onto the East Fork Mill Creek Road and go about 1.5 miles to the trailhead, by the gate to the inholder's castle, at 5600ft.

Route
Follow the trail to Elbow Lake: it's mostly gentle and smooth up to the pass at 8300ft and down to the creek, then rocky with wet or muddy sections

Mount Cowen from the east.

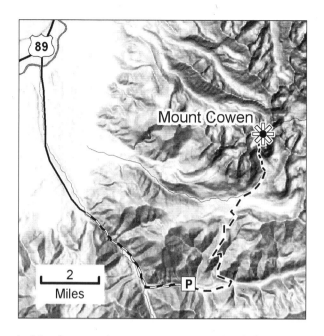

back up to the lake. (At a post by a wet spot in a meadow before the pass, go straight; do not switchback left.) There are many well-used but still nice campsites, especially on the south side.

Cross the outlet and follow a climbers trail, interrupted by occasional talus, along the west side of the lake and up along the gorgeous inlet stream into the alpine world.

The Cowen basin is characterized by cliffs and ledges of monolithic granite. The 'cliffs' are of varied heights and are often laid back some; the 'ledges' are sometimes bare and wide, sometimes narrow and talus-covered, and are mixed in with the cliffs helter-skelter. One broad cliff-band separates the basin just above Elbow Lake from an upper basin. This band is most easily passed by talus & veg slopes on the east side. Once above it, stay near the east edge of the upper basin, on talus, slabs and snow, to a small, often icy tarn. Pass the tarn on its west shore and continue N up a 'black dike' couloir to get through the cliff band above. Then traverse right into another black dike couloir that angles right and climbs to a notch at the base of Cowen's west ridge. There's no exposure and just talus and a bit of somewhat loose and grungy scrambling to this spectacular point.

The route up the SW face to the ledge on the E face is fairly well cairned—take your time to look both for cairns and the obvious route. As always, remember to zig before you zag.

The final 20ft is harder climbing and much more exposed. The 'summit' is the northern most block—a surprisingly large & flat spot with two old pipe registers. Perhaps 40ft to the south is a pointy 'flake' that may jut up a few inches higher; and in between are a couple of other slightly lower blocks. From the ledge, you need to figure out whether and how to go any further.

Mount Edith (9,507ft — p 4,080ft)

Status
>Highpoint of the Big Belt Mountains
>Broadwater & Meagher County HP & BP
>Prominence rank = 12

Difficulty
>Half-day hike on trail and easy cross-country
>7 miles RT with 2300ft gain from the 7250ft saddle
>Subtract 2 miles and 400ft gain if you drive to the TH
>Add 6 miles RT with 1100ft gain for Mt Baldy

Other sources
>Websites: Summitpost, County Highpointers
>Books: HGM79, HM04, B-B

Land status
>Helena NF

Although the lower slopes are clothed with an overstory of dead & dying pine, all the young trees and lovely flowers make this a pretty hike. If you have binoculars be sure to check out all the glinting white "rocks" to see if any of them are furry.

Driving

The Cabin Gulch Road leaves US 12 about 15 miles east of Townsend. Head north on this narrow but scenic and mostly smooth logging road for 9 miles to a

View of Mount Baldy and Edith Lake from Mount Edith.

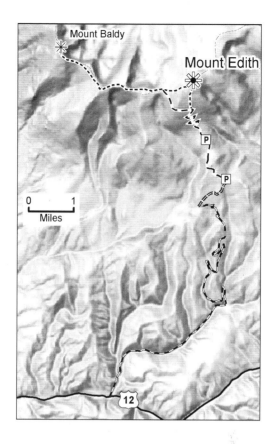

saddle and junction. (Continuing straight ahead takes you into the N Fk of Deep Creek and eventually back to US 12.) Turn right onto a poorer quality road and go another mile to a clearing in a saddle. I usually park here at 7250ft but with care a 2WD vehicle can go another mile to the current trailhead on the north side of an open blip at 7640ft.

Route

Continue up the old track, past the old trailhead and into the switchbacks. At the last switchback, where the trees thin a bit and you can just see open veg & talus slopes above, leave the trail and head up those slopes, veering right as you get higher to reach the broad, gentle summit.

From the shale-rock summit head west along the open crest, enjoying (hopefully) the lupinus aroma, and drop to the granitic saddle and trail. Turn left and walk back to your vehicle—OR—

The traverse over to Mt Baldy (9472+ft, second-highest in the range) is highly recommended—it's pretty and scenic and mostly pleasant walking. Just stay on the crest, except where the rocks and krumholz force you onto the S & W sides in a couple of places. Note that Baldy's bench mark is located on the ridge about 100 feet before you reach the highpoint.

Mount Jefferson (10,203ft — p 3,363ft)

Status

Highpoint of the Centennial Mountains
Prominence rank = 37

Difficulty

Bit of trail, bit of moderate bushwhacking, mostly open cross-country
9 miles RT with 3800ft gain
North ridge has 30 feet of steep, exposed, somewhat rotten 3rd class;
east ridge is just a walk.

Other sources

Books: EIM

Land status

Beaverhead-Deerlodge NF

The eastern end of the Centennial Mountains (or "Eastern Centennials" on some maps) has three main uplifts: Baldy Mountain south of Lower Red Rock Lake, Taylor (& Sheep) Mountain south of the Upper Lake, and Mt Jefferson at the far east end, south of Red Rock Pass. The whole range is gentle on the south and steeper on the north, and the Idaho side has lots of ORV use and terracing to try to curb erosion from past over-grazing. Jefferson has the best views and scenery, in spite of nearby Sawtell Peak with its huge FAA dome. It is most easily climbed from the road up Sawtell, or from a camp in upper Hell Roaring Creek. But the route described below is really fun and scenic.

Mount Jefferson (far left) from its NE cirque.

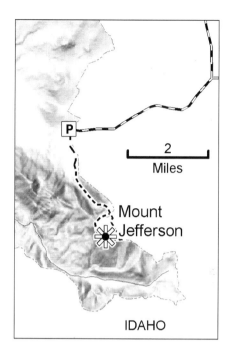

Driving

Go south of Raynolds Pass into Idaho and turn west onto Henrys Lake Road (signed for Red Rock Lakes NWR). The pavement stops at Frome County Park (free camping). Go 10 miles total up to Red Rock Pass and turn south on a dirt track (the CDT) by the Continental Divide sign at 7140ft. Park wherever—there's no actual trailhead, but the track ends in about 100 yards.

Route

Follow the CDT south as it weaves up through woods for about a mile, to where it turns sharply west and levels out. Leave the trail and bushwhack east to the top of the little ridge and follow it south until it disappears into a steep slope heading up to the east. At this point you have a choice: climb the steep slope, which becomes a ridge and then opens into talus, and follow it over a blip to a large veg plateau at 9500ft; OR contour south into the bottom of Cole Creek, looking for and following the sweet spot at the base of the talus, and then head up the drainage and its steep, wooded headwall to the same plateau. (I prefer the Cole Creek route—it's really pretty, and talus is hard on old knees.) At the south edge of the plateau, looking over the rubbly basin NE of the peak, you again have a choice. Experienced scramblers and hikers who aren't afraid to die can follow the ridge (Continental Divide) over one limy blip and down to the base of a 30ft high step that is steep and somewhat loose but goes with no hard moves, just some exposure. Sensible folk will want to drop into the basin and pick a route over to the veg ramp that climbs to a saddle on Jefferson's east ridge, then follow the ridge easily to the top. Expect some loose scree, and watch out for moose and bear.

Mount Powell (10,168ft — p 3,728ft)

Status
>Highpoint of the Flint Creek Range
>Powell County HP & BP
>Prominence rank = 26

Difficulty
>Day hike on old road/ORV route and cross-country
>6 miles one-way with 4000ft gain, or
>14 miles RT with 5100ft gain (includes walking 2+ miles of road)
>With care you can avoid any serious bushwhacking

Other sources
>Websites: County Highpointers
>Books: WM, CGM

Land status
>Beaverhead-Deerlodge NF

The Flints, like most mineralized ranges, have a plethora of old roads and tracks and the ORV use they invite. Most of the lakes have small dams to prolong summer stream flows for irrigation. But there remain a few wild spots, and the highest peaks are among them. Mount Powell dominates the range, and its NE cirque is spectacular.

Access from the east is restricted by the presence of the Montana State Prison to two routes: FS Road # 5149 on the north and FS Road # 8507 on the south. The former is less used and a bit shorter; but the road is really bad. The southern route, up Dempsey Creek, also offers a reasonable loop hike over Deer Lodge Mountain; so it's the one I describe below.

View of Mount Powell and "The Crater" from Deer Lodge Mtn.

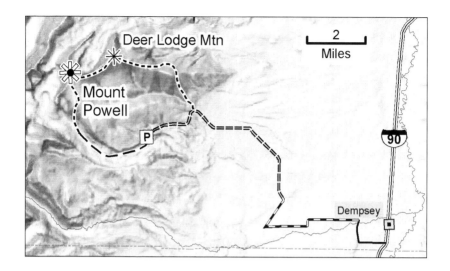

Driving

There are many combinations of county roads that will get you to Dempsey Creek; here's one. Exit I-90 at Racetrack (#195). Go west one mile to a 'T'. Turn right (N) and go 0.7 mile to gravel Quinlan Road. Go west, with a dogleg south, 3.5 miles. Turn sharp right and go NE a long mile to a 'Y'. Turn left and after 100 yards branch right up the hill on FS Road # 8507. Follow this road about 7.5 miles to the ORV trailhead at 6200ft. [NOTE: parts of the 5 miles through the state prison ranch are really soft and greasy when wet.]

If you plan to hike the loop, you'll end up about 2.5 miles back down the road, where it crosses the North Fork; so you might park there and walk up the road in the morning (or bring two vehicles or a bike).

Route

Walk up the rocky old road/ATV route, marveling that people drive it for fun, about 3.5 miles to an ATV bridge over the creek. Don't cross the creek, but do cross the small stream that feeds into it a few yards up and continue up through fairly open woods, aiming for the steep rocky prow of the ridge to its west. At the base of the rocks, find a good game trail that traverses up the west side of the drainage, above the gnarly bottom, to the plateau at 8600ft. Then just head up the south slopes of the mountain to the summit. The ridge route over to Deer Lodge Mountain is obvious and mostly pleasant, with wonderful views of "The Crater", as is the descent of its ESE ridge. There is some deadfall, and talus on and near Pt 8590. From the saddle east of that point, pick up a good game trail on the north side and follow it down and around Pt 8266, to avoid the extensive talus there. Then drop steeply down through mostly open woods, heading SE towards the big, meadowy bench and Road # 8507 below.

Mount Wood (12,649+ft — p 2,809ft)

Status
> Stillwater County HP & BP
> Elevation rank = 2
> Prominence rank = 62

Difficulty
> Backpack 6 miles on trail with 1400ft gain to camp
> Day hike cross-country about 4 miles one-way with 5000ft gain
> Some strenuous talus and easy scrambling in the summit area

Other sources
> Websites: County Highpointers
> Books: SPGY

Land status
> Custer NF, Absaroka-Beartooth Wilderness

"Granite Range" is the name given to the high country N of West Rosebud Creek. Most of the rock is actually metamorphic, but this area is indeed rocky: even the drainages are choked with talus. It's only a minor subrange of the Beartooths, but it does include the state's 2nd highest peak, Mt Wood.

Mt Wood has two summits. The lower west peak is sharper and has the better view. It has a spot elevation of 12,649ft (12,661ft on FS maps and the old 15 minute topo). The higher east peak is a mini-plateau and has no spot elevation; so I list Mt Wood as 12,649+ft.

Although people often climb Wood from the north, I think the southern route is nicer. It is 5000ft and 4 miles up from camp at Mystic Lake, but most of that ground is pleasant walking with wonderful views.

Driving

From MT 78 a few miles south of Absarokee, head west on SR 419. One mile past Fishtail, turn left onto the West Rosebud Road. After another 6.5 miles, the pavement ends at a fork—drop left down to the creek and continue another 14 miles to the TH just before the PPL-MT facility at 6600ft.

Mount Wood from the south.

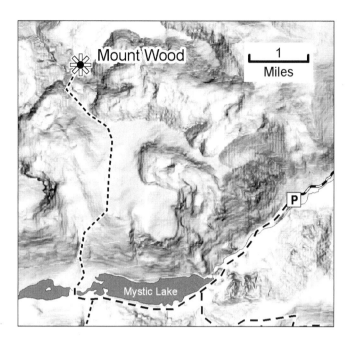

Route

Hike up the trail to the dam and continue around the lake across Huckleberry Creek and up to the log-jam at the outlet of Island Lake. Cross over (it goes even in high water) and immediately head downstream on a use trail, then swing N to camping in open lodgepole pine woods by the creek draining the SW side of Mt Wood.

You want to get on the E side of the creek and a good game trail above 8000ft. The creek is easier to cross down low, but the east side is pretty gnarly down low too.

Where the slope breaks (ca. 9200ft) bend R up the ridge, aiming for the highest trees to the left. A thread of veg then leads straight up to the left of some low cliffs onto the plateau at 10,400ft. From here it's a gentle veg walk N to the basin rim at 11,400ft, and then easy talus to a notch just S of the mountain at 11,800ft.

The route beyond depends on snow conditions and your comfort level on snow. For the easiest route up the west peak, climb to the saddle between the peaks, contour NW across the NE face, then climb a ramp (almost 3rd class) to the top.

For the east peak, stay below the slabby rock and climb talus to the notch just W of the highpoint.

Nasukoin Mountain (8,086ft — p 3,046ft)
and peaks in the Whitefish Range

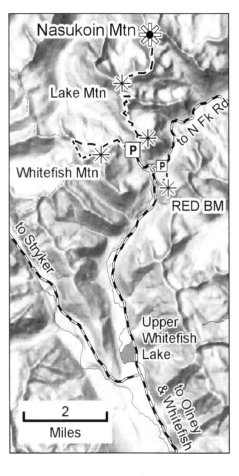

Status
　Highpoint of the Montana portion of the Whitefish Range
　Prominence rank = 49
Difficulty
　Day hike on trail
　5 miles one-way with 3300ft gain
　Grizzly bear area!
Other sources
　Books: WM
Land status
　Flathead NF

This is a wonderful hike. The trail is excellent, even on its improbable plunge down the east face of Lake Mountain. The scenery starts out very nice and then goes to "wow". Unfortunately, you do have to climb Lake Mountain twice; but it's still just 3300 feet of total gain, and having to spend extra time in this wild country isn't so terrible. Nasukoin is pretty remote, and you'll encounter some rough sections of road getting there; so plan on spending a few days and bagging other peaks in the area.

The Whitefish Range extends north into British Columbia, where it rises to 8,740 feet at Mount Doupe and merges with the northern end of the Livingston Range.

Driving

Red Meadow Lake, campground, and pass can be reached from either the North Fork Flathead River on the east or from Whitefish, Olney or Stryker on the west. The road up Red Meadow Creek is the nicest (it's 12+ miles); but there are several bone-jarring sections on the North Fork road getting to it. The route from Olney has the least amount of gravel, but it's really rocky and has bad potholes north of Upper Whitefish Lake. Road #589, a good though occasionally steep road, takes off about 0.1 mile west of the pass and ends in 1.5 miles at the TH in a saddle at 6000ft.

Nasukoin Mountain (in the clouds) from the south.

Route
Hike up the trail to a junction in the saddle above Link Lake, turn north and follow the trail over Lake Mountain to Nasukoin Mountain

Other Peaks
Visiting the Nasukoin area is an obvious add-on to a climb of Kintla Peak from either Kintla or Bowman Lakes. Besides Nasukoin and Lake Mountains, three other peaks in the immediate area are fun climbs. The small (free) campground at Red Meadow Lake is an excellent base for all of these hikes.

Link Mountain (7227ft — p 600ft)
In the saddle above Link Lake an old trail takes off just across from the sign at the trail junction and heads SE up the ridge.

Whitefish Mountain (7417ft – p 1400ft)
From the TH for Nasukoin, follow trail #26 west to the mountain's NW ridge then head up the ridge to the top.

RED BM (7601ft – p 1990ft)
From the campground, bushwhack up into the veg bowl on the north face then cut right to the NW ridge and follow it to the top.

Northwest Peak (7,705ft — p 4,424ft)
and the Libby area

Status
>Highpoint of the southern Purcell Mountains
>Prominence rank = 6

Difficulty
>Half-day hike on trail
>2 miles one-way with 1600ft gain

Other sources
>Books: HGM79&94, HM04, CGM, WM

I really debated about whether to include this one—but how can one ignore 4400 feet of prominence? Still, it's a really long drive, mostly in a tree-tunnel, for a very short and not that interesting hike. The woods are green and lush, and the many larch are especially lovely in spring and fall; but the few views are underwhelming: rounded ridges with clearcuts.

The summit area is nice—granite talus with wind-sheared larch, and the trail is pleasant. But really, this hike only makes sense if you spend additional time bagging other peaks in the Yaak, peaks with longer and more interesting routes. Here's a good multi-day loop starting from Libby: O'Brien Mountain, then Roderick

View north from the slopes of Northwest Peak.

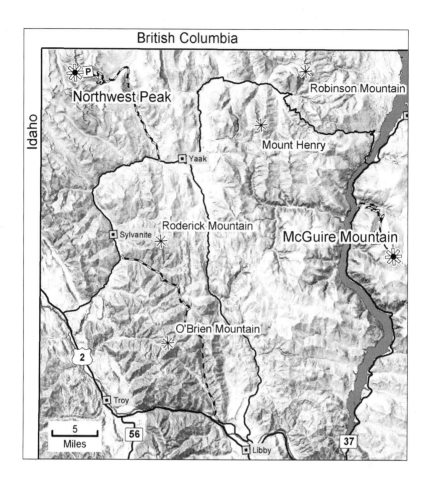

British Columbia

Northwest Peak

Idaho

Robinson Mountain

Mount Henry

Yaak

Roderick Mountain

Sylvanite

McGuire Mountain

O'Brien Mountain

2

Troy

5
Miles

56

Libby

37

Mountain, then Northwest Peak, then Mt Henry, then Robinson Mountain, and end with McGuire Mountain (see page 74). Stop at a FS Ranger Station and ask for handouts on the trails up these peaks.

Note that the Purcell Mountains are located mainly in British Columbia, where they rise to 11,342ft at Mount Farnham and include the Bugaboos and other famous climbing areas.

Driving

A paved road, MT 508 on the west and FS Road #92 on the east, runs for 73 miles between US 2 north of Troy and the Lake Koocanusa bridge and MT 37 south of Rexford. At MP 27, a few miles west of Yaak, the Pete Creek Road (FS # 338) heads north. Follow this mostly good road for just under 20 miles to the trailhead at 6300 feet.

Route

Hike up the obvious trail to the old lookout on top.

O'Brien Mountain (6772ft — p 3112ft)
about 6 miles one-way with 4000ft gain

Trail #13 (part of the Skyline NRT) is a wonderful hike, though the trail is in bad shape. It starts in old-growth cedar along the West Fork of Quartz Creek and climbs up through varied forests to the open slopes of the peak. The summit ridge is scarred by old bulldozer tracks that switchback up out of Seventeenmile Creek; but it's still a lovely place.

FS Rd #600 runs from the Kootenai River NW of Libby north to the 17 Mile Rd (#471). Roughly 5 miles north of the river, veer left onto Road #399, cross Quartz Creek and continue past Road # 4654 to a "T" just across the West Fork. Turn right and go up about 1/2 mile to a switchback just before a gate and park at 3100ft. A newer trail drops down to the creek and crosses a bit upstream to join the original.

Cedar grove, West Fork of Quartz Creek, O'Brien Mountain.

Roderick Mountain (6644ft — p 2304ft)
about 4 miles one-way with 4000ft gain

Trail #19 leaves the "17 Mile Rd" at MP 12.1 (3.6 miles east of the Yaak Hwy)—look for the sign high up the slope. It climbs steeply up a spur ridge and into a burn. Where it starts dropping gently across the east slope, I'd suggest bushwhacking on up the ridge to the old lookout site at Pleasant View Mountain. You'll have some deadfall in the burn; but the trail, besides dropping some, can

Looking southwest from Roderick Mountain, Pleasant View Mountain on the right.

be hard to follow and may have a bunch of deadfall too. From Pleasant View, pick up the trail on the open east side of the ridge and follow it to the south slopes of Roderick Mountain.

Mount Henry (7243ft — p 1743ft)
about 6.5 miles one-way with 4000ft gain

Trail #9 heads east up Vinal Creek through lovely forests before climbing the west ridge and face of the peak to the old lookout and some great views. You do cross or briefly join some old logging roads on the ridge and go through burned areas too; but this is still a very scenic hike.

From the community of Yaak, go 4 miles south on the paved road to Libby, then turn left and go 5 miles north on Road #746 to the TH on the north side of Vinal Creek at 3100ft.

Robinson Mountain (7539ft — p 3639ft)
about 4 miles one-way with 2400ft gain

This is another poorly maintained trail to an old lookout site, with some mix of old road and trail through logged areas at the start, then lovely country and walking with great views up high. I haven't been up here since 1985—but hopefully these directions will get you to the trail! Go north on the paved west side (of Koocanusa) road (FS #474) about 2 miles past the junction with Road #92, veer left onto Road #470 and follow it about 8 miles to Road #7205, turn right and go about 1.7 miles and look for the trail/old road on the left.

Peak E of Quigg Peak (8,468ft — p 2,548ft)

Status
    Highpoint of the John Long Mountains area
    Prominence rank = 81
    Granite County BP
Difficulty
    Long day hike on little-used trail
    7.5 miles one-way with 5000ft gain
    Parts of the trail are steep, parts rocky
Other sources
    Books: WM
Land status
    Lolo NF

This peak is often called Burnt Cabin Ridge. It's not clear from maps that the name John Long Mountains includes the Quigg Peak area; but I do so here. These are gentle mountains cut by steep-sided drainages that have an astonishing amount of exposed rubble/talus. The Quigg Peak area has an extensive network of trails, several of which access the highpoint. I think the Hogback Ridge trail is the easiest and most scenic.

Driving

From the Rock Creek exit on I-90, drive slowly up Rock Creek about 30 miles to the trailhead and cabin site at 4520ft.

From Philipsburg, follow MT 348 west for 14 miles to the end of the pavement at Rock Creek. Turn right and drive downstream about 12 miles to the trailhead.

Near start of Hogback Ridge Trail to Pk E of Quigg.

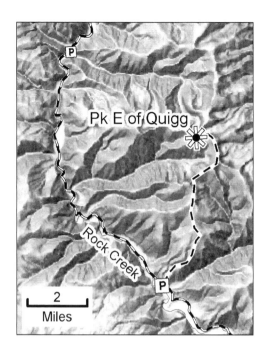

Route

The trail now has very gentle switchbacks at the start, allowing more time to enjoy the gorgeous scenery. But after a mile or so it heads straight up the ridge before gentling-out at about 7500ft. It's then a delightful walk through open forest along the ridge. At 6 miles there's a signed junction with the trail to Hogback Point, beyond which you enter a small 2007 burn and the trail gets rockier. When you hit the saddle below the peak, just head west up the slope and you'll soon cut the Burnt Cabin Ridge trail. Turn right and follow it up through two switchbacks; then either bushwhack up the east face of the peak or follow the trail across to the gentler but rocky north ridge. The open, rubbly summit affords wide-ranging views and a great view of the main Bitterroots.

For a shorter hike, stay on the trail until it drops to the saddle just north of Peak 8322 (about 5.5 miles up)—you'll get good views here, and can bushwhack SW up the ridge if you want to bag a peak.

Alternate route

From I-90 take the Rock Creek road about 19 miles south to Burnt Cabin Creek and park at 4160ft. Walk up the old road, past the gate and gravel pit and along the reclaimed road a short mile to a stream crossing—the one and only if hiking the ridge trail (#227), the first of many if going up the creek (#224). Either way you'll enjoy miles (and miles and miles) of wild and little-used country.

Peak S of Sheep Mountain
(10,606ft — p 3,666ft)

Status
> Highpoint of the Henrys Lake Mountains
> Prominence rank = 28

Difficulty
> Day hike mostly on trail
> 12 miles RT with 4500ft gain—less if you don't do Coffin Mountain
> Bridged creek crossings and mostly open cross-country travel

Other sources
> Books: WM

Land status
> Gallatin NF

The Henrys Lake Mountains are geologically and topographically part of the Madison Range, but cut off from it by the Madison River. There is lots of vehicle-based recreation in the range, but only mountain bikes in Sheep Creek. This route can be an in & out hike, but the partial loop over Coffin Mountain is scenic and special—its limy open slopes are such a contrast with the broken metamorphic landscape of the canyon and west-side ridge. There is limited camping below the outlet of Sheep Lake, much more farther down the canyon.

Pk S of Sheep Mtn (far right) from Sheep Lake.

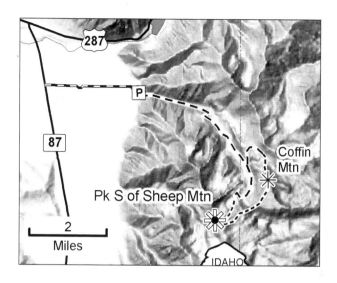

Driving

From US 287 head south on MT 87 about 1.4 miles towards Raynolds Pass to the Sheep Creek Road on the east. Follow this road about 2.6 miles to its end at the trailhead (and possible camping) at 6500ft.

Route

This lovely, well-maintained trail climbs up along Sheep Creek through a lush and rocky section and into some broad meadows before looping around the head of the drainage and climbing steeply to Sheep Lake. From the small dam, work your way around the east shore to the obvious broken rock & veg ramp that stays to the right of the talus and climbs steeply to the ridge—and a totally different world.

On the descent, follow the ridge down to the saddle at the base of Coffin Mtn., where you have two choices. One is to descend north down to the trail, staying as much as possible in the white-bark pine on the west slopes of Coffin Mountain. The other (recommended) option is to follow the obvious game trail up the slope to the left of the short cliff and onto the broad expanse of Coffin Mountain. From the summit, continue north along the rim and drop due north into the woods, aiming for the pond in the meadow at the base of the mountain. At the north edge of this meadow, pick up the trail in the woods—it climbs gently to cross a small ridge before switch-backing steeply down to the main trail.

Pryor Mountains HP (8,790ft or so — p 4,290ft or so)

Status
> Highpoint of the Pryor Mountains
> Prominence rank = 10
> Carbon County BP

Difficulty
> Short trail hike and a short meadow ramble—OR
> 2 full day hikes on ORV routes and bushwhacking

Other sources
> Website: Summitpost

Land status
> Custer NF, BLM, Bighorn Canyon NRA

Bighorn Canyon and the Bighorn Mtns from Layout Creek.

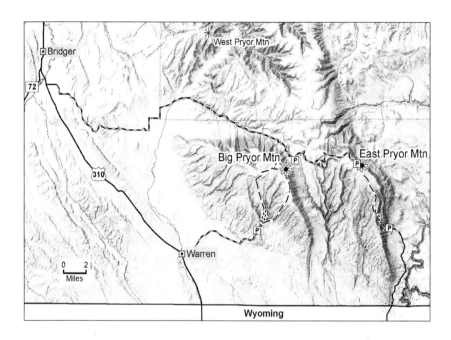

The Pryors are unique in Montana—a bit of Utah's canyon country mixed with high mountain meadows. As discussed under 'close calls', it's really unclear which of three possible locations is the highpoint: the ICE BM on East Pryor Mountain, the ICE CAVE BM on Big Pryor Mountain, or high ground near the SHRIVER BM also on Big Pryor Mountain. So what's the committed peakbagger to do but to climb all three!

The easy ways up both Big Pryor and East Pryor involve driving the main NF access, Pryor Mountain Rd, up past the Sage Creek campground to Tie Flat, and the short trail that switchbacks up to Big Pryor, and then on past Dry Head Vista, to wander up to the East Pryor HP. Both peaks can be bagged in half a day.

However, my two favorite spots in the Pryors are Layout Creek on the east and Bear Canyon on the west. So this guide describes two long day hikes that include those features—ridiculous routes really, but fun hikes if you're in good shape and not very bright.

East Pryor Mountain
An 'in & out' hike of about 16 miles RT with 4500ft gain

Leave US 14A a few miles east of Lovell, WY and head north on WY 37 for about 20 miles to the "Ewing-Snell Ranch" entrance right after crossing Layout Creek. Go through the gate and find the sign for "Upper Layout Creek Trail". Follow the narrow gravel road for 1.4 miles to a small parking area at the mouth of the canyon at 4700ft.

Hike up the signed trail to its end at the 'source'. Now you need to bushwhack

Wild horses on slopes below East Pryor Mtn.

up the canyon about 3/4 miles. Stay near the left (SW) wall until the slope eases. Then find surprisingly good walking up the narrow, rubbly drainage. As you near the west-side exit drainage, things get pretty gnarly, and stay gnarly until you've climbed several hundred feet up its N (south-facing) side. Where it bends N, cross it and continue W to the ridge where, hopefully, you'll hit the Sykes Ridge road in a small, open saddle (~7150ft).

Now walk up the road to the top. If you've started early enough (and this route *demands* an early start) the first part is shady and the second part, in the meadows, is so gorgeous it doesn't matter. The bench mark is in the open, just north of a wire-fenced exclosure, about 1/4 mile south of the radio tower. Drop east 200 yds to an open point with a great view for lunch. Then it's back out! Expect to encounter ORVs and wild horses on this route.

Part of Bear Canyon on the southwest slopes of Big Pryor Mtn.

Big Pryor Mountain
A loop hike of about 16 miles RT with 3500ft gain

From Warren, a bleak industrial site on US 310, head east on Helt Road for 2.7 miles to a fork, stay right (straight) and continue another 3.5 rougher miles to Bear Canyon Road. Very slowly drive this rocky &/or muddy road as far as you can, or can stand to. It's about 2 miles to its end at the NF boundary and lovely camping at 5400ft.

This long loop is almost entirely on ORV routes, except for getting out of and back into Bear Canyon. Avoid weekend traffic if possible, and get an early start—there's very little cover from either sun or afternoon storms. From the roads' end backtrack about 1/8 mile to a break in the east canyon wall. Go up the small drainage and pick up a game trail that heads north and gently up, staying somewhat back from the rim. After crossing the NF boundary fence, continue north through an open saddle and up a game trail along the west side of the pretty horn (Pt 5985)—you'll soon hit an old track which slowly morphs into an ATV trail. Follow this supposedly closed route up the ridge until you're into the broad, gentle meadows. Then angle more N, cut the ridge road, and follow it to the top (cairn with big post, and ICE BM).

It's a pleasant meadow walk on a closed track over to SHRIVER BM (on a large flat area of rock about 200 feet SW of the ill-defined 'summit'). Then head S back to the main road and follow it W, past one route dropping N, to a route dropping S just past a fence-line. Drop down this one, past a spring pond, and look for a little-used track that heads south down the gentle ridge. Follow this until it peters-out after going around the W side of a wooded blip.

You now have two choices: nice but dicey or gnarly but safe.

For nice & dicey, continue on the ridge south then southwest until you come to breaks in the cliffs and can pick a route down to the main branch of the canyon.

For safe & gnarly, follow the drainage that begins just south of the wooded blip and curves west, dissecting the plateau and dropping into the west branch of the canyon.

Once on the bottom, follow an old track out to the NF boundary and your vehicle.

QUARTZ BM (7,770ft — p 1,890ft)

Status
>Highpoint of the Northern Bitterroots in Montana
>Mineral County HP

Difficulty
>Long day hike on trail and abandoned trail
>9 miles one-way with 5400ft gain
>Not as tough as the numbers suggest

Other sources
>Website: County Highpointers

Land Status
>Lolo NF

The highpoint of the Northern Bitterroots is Rhodes Peak (7930ft, p 2690ft), which is located entirely in Idaho. Although the range is heavily roaded and logged, there are still pockets of wild and pristine country along the divide. The largest of those pockets is often called the "Great Burn" (after the 1910 fire that burned three million acres in this part of Idaho & Montana). QUARTZ is on the northern edge of the Great Burn and Rhodes Peak is on the south.

Trail to Pearl Lake, en route to QUARTZ BM.

Though the distant views aren't that great, the near views and immediate scenery are really lovely, especially early and late in the season when snow patches or beginning fall colors accent the landscape.

There are beat-up campsites at Heart Lake and lumpy ones in the beargrass around Pearl Lake. But the best camping, if you want to spend more time enjoying the area's beauty, is along the ridges: either pack water or go when snow banks linger.

Driving

From the south side of I 90 at exit 47 in Superior, head east on Diamond Match Rd, which becomes FS Road # 250. It's 20.5 miles to the trailhead: the first 6 miles are paved, the rest is excellent gravel, though prone to washboard and dust from too many people driving too fast. There is level parking and an outhouse at the trailhead at 4650ft.

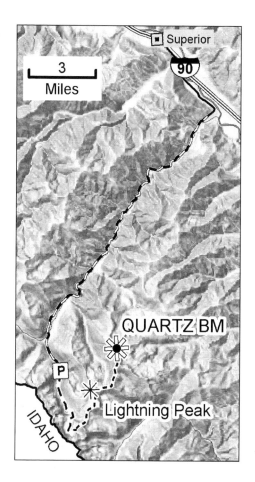

Route

Hike good trail up the drainage to an unsigned junction just across the stream draining Heart Lake. Turn left and follow well-used trail across the lake's outlet, along its east shore and up to Pearl Lake. Notice the blip north of the lake with a cliffy west face. An old trail coming south from QUARTZ crosses above those cliffs, drops to the wooded shoulder to the west and starts switchbacking down towards Pearl Lake—but I'm not sure where it joined the trail you're on. So just bushwhack up the mostly open slope towards that shoulder and you will hit that old trail at some point. Follow it over the blip (a great viewpoint) and north along the ridge (blazes, cut logs, well-worn tread). The stretch from Pt 7082 through the saddle and up to Lightning Peak is mostly gone—either buried in spruce-fir repro or lost on beargrass slopes; so follow game trails and/or the open east edge of the ridge. From Lightning Peak on north the trail is mostly obvious and excellent, though a few spots require some looking. From the saddle just below QUARTZ, where the trail veers off to the right, bushwhack up the east edge of the ridge to the top.

Red Mountain (9,411ft — p 3,801ft)

Status

    Highpoint of the Lewis & Clark Range

    Lewis & Clark County HP & BP

    Prominence rank = 21

Difficulty

    Day hike on old road/ATV route and cross-country

    10 miles RT with 3500ft gain.

    Grizzly bear area!

Other sources

    Websites: Summitpost, County Highpointers

Land status

    Helena NF, on the Scapegoat Wilderness boundary

This is a big, beautiful mountain with long sweeping ridges, terrific views, colorful rocks, craggy slopes, resident mountain goats and delightful hiking. It's lovely in spite of being surrounded by thousands of acres of recent (1988, 2004) burns and extensive logging and salvage in Copper Creek on the south. A trail climbs the north slope above Ringeye Creek; it's about 9 miles one-way from Indian Meadows to the old lookout site on top. But the loop described here approaches out of Copper Basin on the south. It's shorter, steeper and more scenic—and it avoids all the dust and mud and horse traffic on the mainline trail.

Driving

Turn north off MT 200 about 6 miles east of Lincoln at MP 28 and follow the Copper Creek Road (#330) for 14 miles, past the turn off for Indian Meadows and past Copper Creek Campground, to a gate where the road crosses the creek at 6150ft. Drive, if the gate is open, or walk another mile to where the road turns and heads up a ridge and park about 100 yards up, where a track branches off to the right at around 6300ft.

South ridge of Red Mountain.

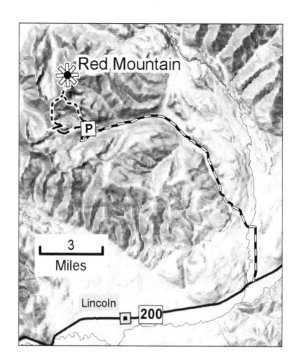

Route

Follow the track through the alders into a drainage, cross the creek and continue through thicker alders then fields of knapweed as the road switchbacks through a small clearcut to the top of a gentle little ridge. Continue west on the ridge out of the burn and steeply up the now-obvious track to its end at an old mine. Bushwhack up the steep ridge above the mine. As you get higher the grade lessens and the mountain's beauty erases all thoughts of knapweed, alder and snags. Stay on the crest until it merges with the broad, open south ridge of Red Mountain, then swing north to the top.

To descend, follow the south ridge back down, but veer west to stay on the main south ridge (and Wilderness Boundary) and go over one big blip and then climb up veggie slopes to the crest of another. Stay right on top here, then zig-zag down some steep ledges to the good game trail that traverses east to a ridge, where you'll find ATV tracks. Follow those tracks down to the mine road that leads back to your vehicle.

Rocky Mountain (9,392ft — p 3,232ft)

Status
> Highpoint of the Sawtooth Range
> Prominence rank = 40
> Teton County HP & BP

Difficulty
> Day hike, partly on trail
> 7 miles RT with 3600ft gain
> Some scree (or snow), some easy scrambling with exposure

Other sources
> Websites: Summitpost, County Highpointers
> Books: DRMF

Land status
> Lewis & Clark NF

The Sawtooth Range, a.k.a. the Rocky Mountain Front, is incredibly scenic at all scales—alpine flowers, mossy alcoves, twisted pines, lush drainages, soaring cliffs, sweeping ridges and valleys, endless prairie, and endless beauty. The range is almost all limestone, which can make for rough going but generally yields smooth trails, stable talus, and pleasant bushwhacking. The terrain often appears intimidating but turns out to be less difficult than it looks. The hike up Rocky Mountain is typical for climbs in the range, in terms of difficulty and rewards. The range offers many other fine peaks to climb: Fairview Mountain, Arsenic Peak, Castle Reef, Ear Mountain, and Mt Wright are some of the more popular ones. (*see photos on pages 5 and 14*)

Driving
From US 89 about 5 miles N of Choteau, head west on paved Teton Canyon Rd 17 miles to the Bellview Cutacross. Turn left, cross the river, then right onto the South Fork Rd and follow it 10 miles to its end at the large trailhead area for Headquarters Pass and Our Lake at 5800ft. (no camping!)

Route
The Headquarters Pass trail provides access to three routes up Rocky Mountain, the east ridge, north ridge and west face.

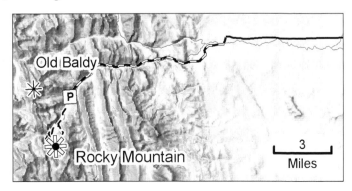

East Ridge route:

The most direct, quickest and most scenic, it's especially nice in winter through mid-June when snow conditions are good (though the ridge itself can be more difficult and exposed then.) Hike the trail until you cross the creek between the two waterfalls. About 20 yards further, at a wooden bridge with a fine view of the upper falls, go straight (SE) on a goat/climber trail up a slot heading directly for the east peak (Peak 9147—3rd highest in the range). After breaking out into the 'east peak ski bowl', head SW up to the rounded spur ridge that climbs steeply to the saddle between the east peak and Rocky Mountain. Pick up another goat/climbers trail that heads west up the ridge, zigzagging through the small cliffs (though not without the occasional use of hands and some exposure).

West Face route:

This is the least intimidating route and the longest. Follow the trail through Headquarters Pass and down the other side until it hits the drainage and swings north. Continue south up to the saddle, then turn east and pick your route up the face. The open gully is easy but loose; its sides are more solid, requiring some use of hands.

North Ridge route:

This is the most exposed and difficult, but still not that hard. From Headquarters Pass just follow the ridge south, staying on the crest. If and when it gets too steep or exposed for you, move into one of the grooves on the east side of the ridge and take it up to the top. NOTE: if you can see snow in these grooves when you enter the basin below the pass, use the east ridge or west face route instead.

The north ridge route is best going up while the others work up or down, so various loops are possible.

Old Baldy (9156 ft — p1356 ft)

Old Baldy is the second highest in the range, and a fun bushwhack. From the TH, backtack 1/4 mile to the creek that drains the mountain's south side. Just head up the creek all the way, curving north into the saddle between Old Baldy's twin summits. This hike is best on good snow or later in the year, when the creek is low. For some fun scrambling with an occasional easy 3rd class move, consider descending the south ridge, following the divide over Peak 8466 and down to the saddle, then heading east on a use trail down to Our Lake and on out the FS trail.

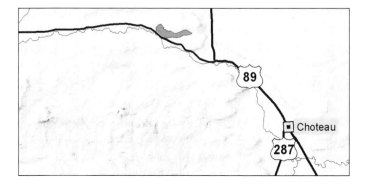

RUBY BM (9,391ft — p 2,431ft)

Status
> Highpoint of the Ruby Range
> Prominence rank = 94

Difficulty
> Day hike partly on old tracks
> 9 miles RT with 3800ft gain
> The canyons and ridge are delightful; getting from one to the other is a grunt

Other sources
> - none

Land status
> BLM, WSA

The Rubies have an igneous core surrounded by limestone canyons. It's dry country with a 'basin & range' feel more like Nevada than Montana, and the northern part especially is little visited. From RUBY south, the range changes character and becomes much gentler and more open.

Driving

In Alder on MT 287, turn west for "Ruby Dam" and then west again in 1/3 mile for the "Alder Bridge/Ruby Island" fishing access. Take this gravel road 2 miles due west to the BLM gate by the entrance to "Spring Canyon Estates". Go through the gate and another 0.9 miles and park where the road dips into dry Porier Gulch at 5600ft.

Hiking this loop requires walking 1.5 miles of road up to the mouth of Laurin Canyon at 6000ft. If you prefer to do an in & out, Porier is the nicer canyon—better trail and more scenic. But Laurin does have water, and the "Y" at its mouth is the best place to camp.

Route

From the mouth of Laurin Canyon, head up the bottom on an old track. This track actually goes 2+ miles up, sometimes in the bottom, sometimes on benches on the south side; but it's pretty gnarly with brush and deadfall in places—look for game trails too. Stay in the bottom until you're 1/2 mile past the spring above the big meadow. [NOTE: to climb Laurin Peak (Peak 9242) too, just head NW up the drainage from the big meadow at 7600ft. From that peak you can easily, albeit with some up & down, follow the crest south to RUBY.] Head west up the slope to the crest, then follow the crest south (look for good game trails) to the summit.

There are several ways to get into Poirier Canyon, but the nicest is to follow the ridge that curves east to the base of Pt 8646 and then drop due N. When things get gnarly, move onto the west-side of the small gully along the slope break and you'll soon pick up an old trail that feeds into the old track in the bottom of the canyon. It's then a delightful walk down the dry canyon on good trail/old track, through a couple of short 'narrows' and out to your vehicle.

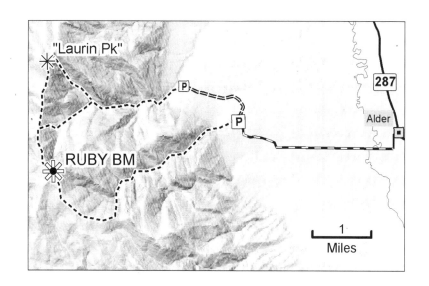

North ridge of RUBY BM.

Sacagawea Peak (9,666ft — p 3,946ft)

Status
> Highpoint of the Bridger Range
> Prominence rank = 19
> Gallatin County BP

Difficulty
> Half day hike on trail
> 2+ miles one way with 2000ft gain OR
> Day hike on old road and trail
> 4.5 miles one way with 4800ft of gain

Other sources
> Websites: Summitpost
> Books: B-B,DHB,CGM,HGM94,HM04

Land status
> Gallatin NF

The Bridgers are basically one big limestone reef—a long ridge of sedimentary rock that is tilted up on the east, so that the east side is cliffy and the west side is slopey. Sacagawea Peak is the highest of many blips along this ridge. Although the range is very narrow and surrounded by rural and suburban development, the Bridgers are quite scenic and the views from the crest are wonderful.

Driving

From near milepost 21.5 on MT 86 between Bozeman and Wilsall, take a rough road 6+ miles west to Fairy Lake and the trailhead at 7700ft.

Route

The trail up to the saddle is often a braided network of trails—but pick the gentlest and you'll have more time to enjoy the incredible scenery. Though it's not immediately obvious, six trails converge in the saddle. The trail to Sacagawea

Sacagawea Peak from the east, Fairy Pass on the right.

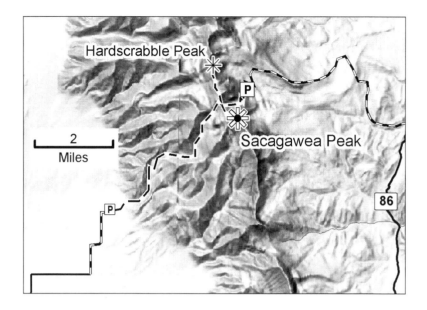

Peak heads south up the crest, gently at first then quite steeply to the top in about 1/2 mile. Another trail heads north up the crest for a long mile to Hardscrabble Peak, second highest in the range at 9,575ft. On the west side are three trails: one contours south towards Ross Peak, one contours north to North Cottonwood Creek and one drops gently (at first) into Corbly Gulch.

Corbly Gulch

The trail up Corbly Gulch is much longer and harder than the standard route from Fairy Lake, and you may encounter ORVs. But it provides an easy west-side access, and it's wild and much less crowded.

Driving

From exit 305 on I 90, take Springhill Road north for 9 miles to Springhill Community Rd, go east for 1.5 miles to Corbly Gulch Rd, then north and east for 2 miles of OK gravel road to a badly eroded dirt track that provides access to the national forest. Park by a cattle guard just 100 yards in at 4900ft.

Route

Walk up the track about a mile to the fence marking the NF boundary, then another mile through lovely park-like woods, with one creek crossing, to where the "trail" branches left, drops down to the creek, and morphs into a real trail. Continue up the drainage with several more creek crossings, through a scruffy area hard-hit by spruce budworm, and finally break into lovely meadow country below the pass and junction with the summit trail.

Snowshoe Peak (8,738ft — p 5,418ft)

Status
> Highpoint of the Cabinet Mountains
> Lincoln and Sanders County HP & BP
> Prominence rank = 3

Difficulty
> Day hike partly on trail
> Some exposed but moderate 3rd class scrambling

Other sources
> Websites: Summitpost, County Highpointers

Land status
> Kootenai NF, Cabinet Mountains Wilderness

The Cabinet Mountains encompass the main range, which includes Snowshoe Peak and which is largely protected as Wilderness, and three major subranges:

The West Cabinets comprise the large area located west of Bull River and Lake Creek. The highpoint, Scotchman Peak (7,009ft—p 4649ft), and most of the subrange is in Idaho.

The eastern-most portion, which I call the Thompson Peak area, is located between the Thompson River and Little Bitterroot River. Its highpoint, Baldy Mountain, is described on page 22.

The southern Cabinets comprise the area south of the Vermilion River and west of the Thompson River. The highpoint is Mount Headley (7,427ft— p3700ft).

The eastern and southern subranges are rather subdued and have been extensively roaded and logged. The main Cabinets are about as wild and woolly as they come. At the Cabinet Mtns. pull-off on MT 56, you're looking at 6400 feet of relief, and most of it is pretty darn gnarly. Routes up Snowshoe from the west are real grunts, especially compared to the elegant NE ridge. But both approaches offer unique challenges and rewards to the peakbagger.

NE Ridge route

From US 2 about 7 miles south of Libby, head SW on Bear Creek Rd. for 3 miles, then right onto FS Road # 867 for 4.5 miles and finally 1.8 miles up to the Leigh Lake TH at 4000ft.

Head up the trail to the lake—staying on the north side of the creek. A fisher/climber trail leads through brush to more open ground.

NE ridge of Snowshoe Peak.

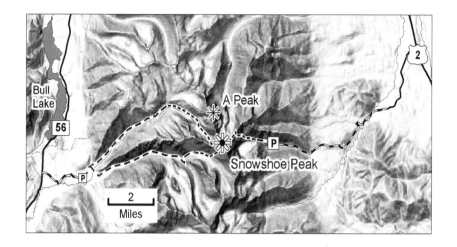

Then pick a route, depending in part on snow conditions, up to the NE ridge—and don't be afraid to take on the cliff band; it's a good warm-up for what's to come. The ridge is glorious, an incredible setting for wonderfully diverse terrain: slabs, cliffy steps, scree gullies, even some gentle snow. There are some solid 3rd class sections, but the route is never intimidating, just fun.

West-side routes

One real advantage to a west-side route is driving MT 56, at least the southern, Bull River, part: it is simply gorgeous. Leave MT 56 at about MP 17 and head east on the "S Fk Rd" (South Fork of Bull River) about 2 miles to a new (2010) bridge at 2400ft. The trail to the Middle Fork and North Fork canyons takes off on the west side of the bridge; parking is on the east side.

The easiest route up Snowshoe is out of the Middle Fork (and in late winter, when you can crampon up to the top!). The maintained trail goes up the north side of the canyon to where Ibex and Bighorn Creeks join just beyond "3rd camp" at 4200ft (campsites are rare in these canyons). But the old trail actually continues another mile and a half: it crosses Ibex Creek, goes several hundred yards up Bighorn Creek to a junction, then switchbacks north back into the Ibex drainage and ends in the meadows on the north side of the creek at 5900ft. From here, simply climb the long slope straight to the top.

If you want to climb A Peak too (8,634ft–p 530ft), you need to go up the North Fork. The maintained trail ends at Verdun Creek, but a use trail (illegally cut-out by fishermen in the mid-1970s) continues up the north side of the creek to Snowshoe Lake. For Snowshoe, the easiest route goes up rubble or snow to its west ridge. For A Peak, head north to the northern of the twin drainages, up that to the bowl, then north again to *its* west ridge. The traverse between the peaks is really fun and has just one or two short cliffs where you'll want a rope. From Snowshoe down to the saddle is basically a walk. Then drop NW on one slanting ramp after another, looking for breaks through to the next, until you hit easier terrain.

Sunset Peak (10,581ft — p 3,741ft)

Status
> Highpoint of the Snowcrest Range (and 'greater Gravelly' area)
> Prominence rank = 24

Difficulty
> Day hike partly on old track
> 10 miles RT with 3800ft gain
> An open grassland hike—tall & thick in the bottom, sparse on top

Other sources
> Book: WM

Land status
> Beaverhead-Deerlodge NF

The Gravelly Mountains are bordered on the west by a narrow band of limestone peaks. The Ruby River cuts this band into two parts: the southern is called the Snowcrest Range and the northern is the Greenhorn Range. The two highest peaks of the entire Gravelly Mountain area happen to be in the Snowcrest Range—Sunset Peak and Hogback Peak. Both are half day hikes from the FS rental cabin in the Notch, but getting to the Notch often requires a 4WD vehicle, and even then can be impassable when wet. (Look up Notch Cabin at www.recreation.gov for information on the route to the cabin.) The route described here is at least accessible via graveled roads—though they are long and rough in places.

Looking SE at Sunset Peak peeking over Pt 9903.

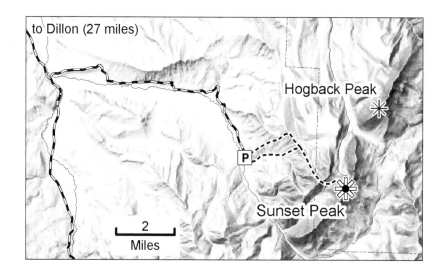

Driving

From Dillon follow the Blacktail Road (on south edge of town, just past the hospital) about 27 miles to the Blacktail WMA entrance. Cross the creek and follow the main, often rocky, road 5.5 miles to a fork where the road to the East Fork campground goes right, crossing the creek. Continue straight ahead and follow the graveled road another 4 miles to its end just before Taylor Creek. You may need a high-clearance vehicle to handle the grassy median strip.

Route

Follow a barely discernible old track from the ranch ruins up along the north side of Taylor Creek. Where the forest starts, head up the first ridge that's in the trees—it climbs east up to a broad, open ridge between Taylor and Rock Creeks. Follow this ridge south then east to the saddle across from (west of) Sunset Peak, drop NE across a scree slope to the base of its NW ridge and head up to the top.

On the descent you can follow the fence line that runs along the ridge north of Taylor Creek all the way down to your vehicle—it's longer, with some up & down, but has better views and hopefully an afternoon breeze.

Table Mountain (10,223ft — p 4,422ft)

Status
> Highpoint of the Highland Mountains
> Silver Bow County HP & BP
> Prominence rank = 7

Difficulty
> Day hike on old tracks and cross county
> 4 miles one-way with 3500ft gain
> Some gnarly deadfall, and route-finding can be tricky on the descent

Other sources
> website: County Highpointers

Land status
> Beaverhead-Deerlodge NF

The rocky-tundra summit bears a solar-powered repeater station, an unfortunate manifestation of our obsession with security and communication. And there are roads and ORV tracks within several miles on all sides. But the high ground and rugged cirques are still wild and scenic.

The shortest route is from the Red Mountain road, which is gated a bit below the old lookout. Walk up past the lookout and simply continue south then east along the crest, often on game/climbers trails, passing over the second highest peak (Peak 10,136) en route to Table Mountain. The entire route is above timber-line. For a more strenuous and adventuresome hike, bushwhack up from the Fish Creek drainage on the north, either past Emerald Lake or along Roaring Brook Ridge. Follow signs to Pigeon Creek campground from a bit east of Pipestone Pass.

The route described here has an occasional stretch of dog-hair or deadfall, but altogether is a delightful ramble in the Boulder Batholith. And the approach on the Hells Canyon road is worth a trip in itself.

Driving

MT 41 crosses the Jefferson River a few miles south of Silver Star. The Hells Canyon Road takes off from the NW end of the bridge, runs south 2 miles to Hells Canyon and then climbs up on the open, scenic benches on the east side of the canyon. Stay on the main road about 15 miles to a fork. The left branch goes downstream to the cabin—take the right branch up along the creek for 1/2 mile to a bridge over a side creek and a nice camp down on the left at 6700ft.

Table Mountain from the south.

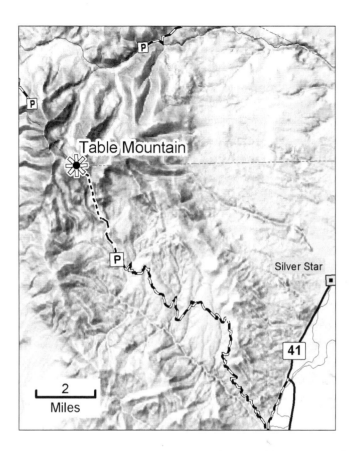

Route

An old track/ATV use-trail heads up the ridge between the two creeks. Where it peters-out in the woods, cross the fence and work north to soon cut a logging road in a little saddle. (You can also drive to this spot by continuing up the road another 3 miles or so—but the route on the ridge is very scenic.) Turn right (east) and walk the road about 100ft past the gate, to where an old track angles left upslope. Follow this track 1/2 mile or less as it slowly disappears—at the end it's just faint motorcycle tracks. Head north up the steep slope to the flats, then angle left along the edge of the flats as they morph into the south ridge of Table Mountain. Once on the ridge, stay on or near the crest all the way, even when the boulders appear to close in on you. They'll almost always part (and if they don't, just skip that section). (NOTE: this route may be marked with cairns and flagging—it is frequently used.)

At about 9000ft the well-defined ridge disappears for about 300ft vertical. Head northwest and mark your route with cairns so you can find the ridge on the way down. (Please knock over your cairns as you descend past them on your return!) The summit area is all quartzite talus. Find game trails up to the plateau along the south edge of the east-face cirque, then pick your way to the top.

Trapper Peak (10,157ft — p3,570ft)

Status
> Highpoint of the Bitterroot Mountains
> Ravalli County HP & BP
> Prominence rank = 32

Difficulty
> Day hike partly to mostly on trail, with some talus
> 4 miles one-way with 3200ft gain

Other sources
> Websites: Summitpost, County Highpointers
> Books: HGM94, HM04, CGM

Land status
> Bitterroot NF, Selway-Bitterroot Wilderness

The main Bitterroots, from Lolo Pass to Lost Trail Pass, cap the eastern edge of the Idaho batholith, a huge mass of granite that extends west almost to Grangeville and south to near Boise. The range was heavily glaciated, resulting in classic mountain scenery: jagged peaks, precipitous walls, slabby lake basins. The glaciers cut back so far to the west that most of the major peaks now lie east of the crest, along ridges separating the long glacial valleys. Several of these high peaks, including Trapper Peak, are accessed by trails up the smooth and relatively gentle east flank of the range (formed when a huge block of overlying Belt rock slid eastward, creating the Bitterroot Valley and Sapphire Range).

There are two easy routes up Trapper. One is the Trapper Peak Trail, which goes almost to the top—there's about 1/4 mile of talus at the end. The other climbs out of the Baker Creek drainage from Gem Lake, reached by climber's trail, and joins the summit trail about 1/2 mile below the top. That route is more scenic and adventuresome, plus it provides access to North Trapper Peak; so that's the route described below.

Trapper Peak (center-right) from the Boulder Point Trail.

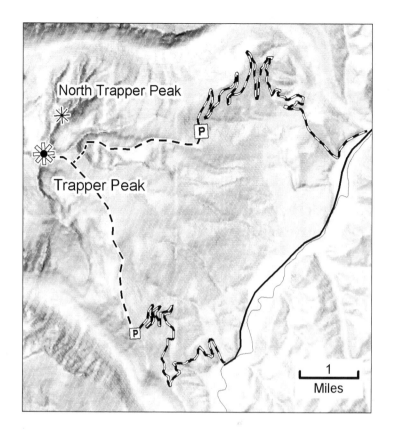

Driving

MT 473 goes up the West Fork Bitterroot River. About a mile past the Job Corps Center, at MP 7, turn right onto FS Road #5634—the Baker Point Rd—and follow it 10 miles to the TH at its end at 7000ft.

Route

Hike the FS trail up to Baker Lake and continue up along the north side of the creek on a well-used climbers trail past Middle Lake (camping) to Gem Lake (camping). Cross the outlet and head south up the obvious gully on slabs, talus and probably snow to the 'plateau'. Then contour around through krumholz and scree until you cut the trail.

North Trapper Peak (9801ft — p 400')

North Trapper Peak is a mostly fun ramble-scramble to an airy summit. It's solid 3rd class with exposure—bring a rope just in case. Start by climbing to the notch north of Gem Lake and descending the rotten couloir on the other side until you can traverse left (west) into the basin below the east face. Head up the basin—a mix of slabs, talus, beargrass and bogs—to near the ugly moraine. Then pick a route north up to the NE ridge and clamber south over airy blocks to the top.

Tweedy Mountain (11,154ft — p 3,794ft)

Status
>Highpoint of the Pioneer Mountains
>Beaverhead County HP & BP
>Elevation rank = 59
>Prominence rank = 22

Difficulty
>Day hike partly on trail, partly bushwhack and talus
>5 miles one-way with 3800ft gain
>Easy bushwhacking and stable, nicely-sized talus

Other sources
>Websites: Summitpost; County Highpointers
>Books: B-B

Land status
>Beaverhead-Deerlodge NF

The Wise River splits the Pioneers into two ranges: the low, gentle and mostly wooded West Pioneers, and the high and craggy East Pioneers. Like many other ranges in SW Montana, the East Pioneers have lots of talus; but unlike those other ranges, the talus in the East Pioneers is actually fun—it's mostly granite (good friction wet or dry) and it's mostly nicely sized and stable.

Both Torrey and Tweedy can be climbed from a camp at Torrey Lake, but I don't like the long hike up David Creek. Tweedy is also often climbed from Barb Lake. Although the route *from* the Lake is a gentle, lovely walk, getting *to* the lake is an occasionally gnarly grunt. So I prefer climbing Tweedy via its NE face from the Gorge Lake trail.

Driving

The worst part of the Tweedy climb is driving the last 3 miles to the trailhead. From the Apex exit on I-15 (#74), go west on the Birch Creek road. Stay right at 8.5 miles and again one mile further to take the Willow Creek road over the hill

NE ramp on Tweedy Mountain.

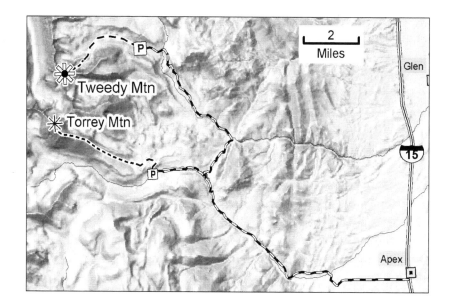

and down to the creek. As the road climbs up along the east side of the creek it slowly gets rockier, narrower and slower. About 16 miles from I-15 take a road branching left that drops to and crosses Willow Creek then contours around to Gorge Creek and goes gently up to the trailhead at the old Winkley Camp at 7450ft, about a mile from the Willow Creek road (if you make it that far!).

Route

The trail to Gorge Lakes is as good as the road is bad. About 3 miles up, where the trail swings south, gentles out and you can hear the creek, look for the old trail (blazes) branching left towards the creek. Follow it 200 yards to a wet meadow, then leave it and head south across the creek, aiming for the obvious break in the cliffs of the ridge to the south. Gain the crest of the ridge and follow it W to the base of the steep veg & talus slope that heads SW then S up to Tweedy's east ridge. Turn right and stroll to the top.

Torrey Mountain (11,147 — p 1,140)
5.5 miles one-way with 4000ft gain

Although there is no data to question Tweedy's primacy, with a mere 7 feet out of 11,000+ separating them it seems only prudent to climb Torrey as well—plus it's a delightful hike.

Return to the Birch Creek Road, turn sharp right and follow it about 2.5 miles to the Dinner Station Camp at 7150ft. Follow the trail about 1 mile up to the old road/ATV route to Deerhead Reservoir. Turn left and go around the south side of the reservoir and continue WSW up to the ridge and on to the top. (The northern branch of Torrey's east ridge is not as nice as the southern.)

West Butte (6,983ft — p 3,953ft)

Status
> Highpoint of the Sweetgrass Hills
> Prominence rank = 31
> Toole County HP & BP

Difficulty
> Half-day hike, no trail
> 3 miles RT with 2600ft gain
> Steep prairie and slide rock slopes laced with game trails

Other sources
> Websites: County Highpointers
> Books: HGM-94

Land status
> State trust land, BLM

The Sweetgrass Hills are not really a mountain range but rather a cluster of isolated buttes surrounded by prairie. West Butte is only slightly higher than the East Butte, which has two peaks: Mount Brown (6,958 ft, p 3198ft, forested summit) and Mount Royal (6,914ft, p 614ft, plastered with towers). Although all of these summits are on public land, they are surrounded by private lands and access can be an issue. You will need to get the landowner's permission to cross private land.

Driving

From Sunburst on I-15, head east on Ninemile Rd about 17 miles to a "T" with Coal Mine Rd at the base of the southwest slopes of West Butte. Park here.

From Galata on US 2, head north on Galata Rd 19 miles, then west on Oilmont Hwy 6 miles, north on Miners Coulee Rd 11 miles and west on Coal Mine Rd about 5 miles, coming in on the right branch of the "T" to the parking spot.
NOTE: all of these "good" county roads can become greasy/squishy when really wet.

West Butte from the southwest.

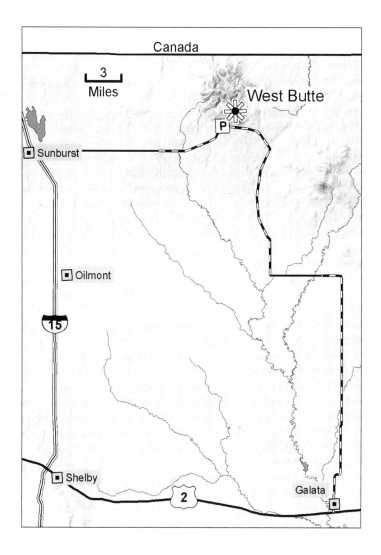

Route

Go up the gentle then steep grassy slope just left (west) of a narrow, rocky gully. Above this prairie section the mountain is a mosaic of forest and rubble. The woods are occasionally gnarly and the rubble is loose, but both are braided with many game trails that really help. Head up generally NE to the gentle grassy summit. Going down can be tricky since it's often hard to tell which direction you're traveling. You might want to use your compass (or GPS) to better aim for your vehicle. You might also consider heading due south from the top, through some tight woods, to the lovely, open, vision-quest site above the south face. Then turn west and descend along the edge of the rocky couloir until a good game trail leads across to the grassy slope you hiked up.

West Goat Peak (10,793ft — p 3,953ft)

Status
>Highpoint of the Anaconda Range
>Deerlodge County HP & BP
>Elevation rank = 94
>Prominence rank = 18

Difficulty
>Day hike partly on trail
>14 miles RT with 4800ft gain
>Some deadfall; loop requires walking ca. 1/2 mile of road

Other sources
>Websites: Summitpost; County Highpointers

Land status
>Beaverhead-Deerlodge NF, Anaconda-Pintler Wilderness

Hiking in the Anaconda Range, or Pintlers, can be a mixed bag: some areas are really pretty and offer delightful routes, while others are scruffy and unappealing with tiresome deadfall, bogs and talus. The loop hike over West Goat described here is kind of in the middle—not as fine as the best of the Pintlers, but never as gnarly as their worst.

West Goat Peak from Hwy 43 (Warren Peak is far left).

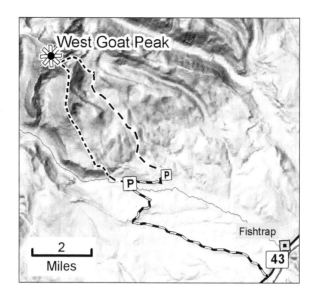

Driving

From MT 43 north of Wisdom turn west onto the NF access road for Fishtrap and Mudd Creeks (about MP 47.5). Go 5.4 miles to a road cutting back to the right and follow this road 2.5 miles to the bridge across the West Fork of Fishtrap Creek and the TH a bit beyond at 6350ft.

For the Middle Fork trail (#129) continue another 1.5 miles, crossing the Middle Fork and passing a track on the right—then look for the trail on the left.

Route

This description is for a clockwise loop—up the south ridge, down past Lost Lakes to trail #129, and out. Later in the season, when the snow is gone from the mountain, you might consider going counter-clockwise—you won't have to deal with snow going up and it's easier dealing with the deadfall on the south ridge going down.

Walk a short mile of trail #130 to just past a creek crossing then head up, staying left of the drainage until the ridge levels out and turns west. Slide through a shallow side drainage and pick up the main ridge again. It's pleasant going for a while but the deadfall slowly gets worse, becoming annoying for several hundred feet (vertical) before the ridge starts to open up. Go up and over East Goat or traverse its west slope, then on up to the top.

Descend the south ridge until you can comfortably drop into lovely Lost Lakes basin. From the outlet of the lower lake, drop down to the equally lovely alpine larch forest and angle SE to the saddle and trail #129. Follow the old blazes carefully, especially up high and through several boggy areas. After a steep drop the trail turns east along the creek. If you're still up for bushwhacking you can cut off a bunch of walking on road by heading due south over lumpy and occasionally gnarly ground until you cut the road perhaps 1/4 mile from the West Fork TH and your vehicle.

Veiw north from Eighteenmile Peak, Beaverhead Mountains. See description on page 42.

View north along the Continental Divide to Eighteenmile Peak.

Montana peak lists

As mentioned in the introduction, there are several types of lists that many peakbaggers like to pursue. The pages that follow present those lists along with small-scale maps showing where the peaks on that list are located. For more extensive lists, consult the websites described in the "Resources" section.

An elevation-based list, like the 100 highest peaks in Montana, is likely the first kind of list that comes to mind. Indeed, it was the first list that I pursued. But after figuring out that most (61) of Montana's 100 highest (p400) peaks are in the Beartooth Mountains, I did start to think about other possible lists. It's not that I dislike the Beartooths; it's just that Montana has an incredible diversity of mountain landscapes and peaks, and I wanted a list that would spur me to explore and experience that full diversity. (Note that as your prominence standard for 'peakhood' decreases, the geographic concentration of your "100 highest" will increase. For example, with a p300 standard, 66 of the 100 highest Montana peaks are in the Beartooths. Conversely, for a p1000 standard, only 23 of the 100 highest are in the Beartooths.)

My favorite kind of list is range highpoints. The peaks on such lists generally provide good geographic and landscape diversity coupled with a lot of prominence. The big problem is the ambiguity in identifying and naming mountain ranges, which leads to a lack of consensus on lists of range highpoints. That can be problematic for peakbaggers who like to tackle well-defined lists or who wish to compare their progress and achievements against those of others.

The first peakbagging book I ever saw (and bought) was "Highpoints of the United States: A Guide to the 50 State Summits" by Don W. Holmes, published in 1990. Pursuing state highpoints was clearly one way to see a lot of different country; so I did. Then, on a big loop trip to climb the Nevada and Arizona highpoints, I came across a new kind of list (for me)—a photocopied sheet stuffed into some summit registers on lesser peaks I climbed along the way. These were lists of the highest peak in each county (for Nevada and Arizona). Well, I thought, that kind of list would clearly provide greater geographic diversity than a 100-highest list and at a finer scale than a list of state highpoints. It might also include isolated but still interesting and worthwhile peaks that are located outside of identified mountain ranges, and indeed it often does.

But the drawback to lists based on administrative boundaries, like state lines or county lines, hit me in the face from the summit of Boundary Peak. That peak is Nevada's highpoint, but it's really just a blip (p 253') on the north ridge of Montgomery Peak in California. And although many county highpoints are really prominent peaks, many are not. In fact, in Montana, the highpoints for four counties are not peaks at all (prominence = 0); they are just spots on a ridge leading up to a peak in an adjoining county. Being a "highpointer" is different from being a "peakbagger".

Mount Cowen (left) viewed from the southwest.

Peaks above Miner Lake Basin, West Big Hole.

There is no ambiguity with lists based on prominence (though there may be issues with data or precision), and clearly no concern with ending up on a blip. Prominence is a totally objective standard, and, as you can see from the map, it produces a nicely dispersed list of peaks. The one problem is that minor ranges, like those in central & eastern Montana, do not get represented. Another problem, at least for an old guy like me coming late into the game, is that Montana's list has way too many tough peaks in Glacier National Park!

Some notes about the tables:

• Peak names in quotation marks are not found on USGS maps or in the GNIS.

• Elevations are from the USGS 7.5 minute topographic maps, except for Electric Peak and Sacagawea Peak (as described in Appendix B).

• All lists are based on a p400 standard. For peaks with less than 400 ft of clean prominence I list the minimum and maximum possible values.

• **Peaks proceeded by "**" are featured in this guide.**

View south from Hilgard Peak, Madison Range.

Montana Peaks over 10,000 feet

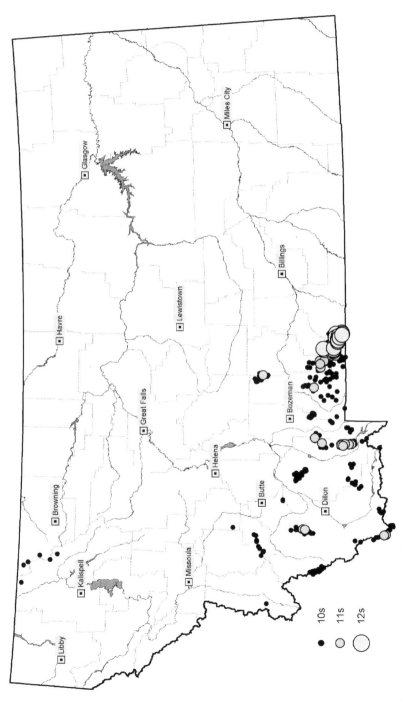

10s
11s
12s

Montana Peaks over 11,000 feet

NOTE: The "elevation" table just lists peaks over 11,000 ft, while the map shows all peaks over 10,000 ft. This is because Montana has 340 peaks over 10,000 ft—too many to list here.

#	MOUNTAIN	ELEV	PROM	RANGE	Date Climbed
1	Granite Peak	12,799	4759	Beartooths	
2	Mount Wood	12,649 +	2809	Beartooths	
3	Castle Mountain	12,612	2652	Beartooths	
4	Whitetail Peak	12,551	1271	Beartooths	
5	Silver Run Peak	12,542	1505	Beartooths	
6	Castle Rock Spire	12,540	460	Beartooths	
7	Tempest Mountain	12,469	909	Beartooths	
8	Mount Peal	12,409	489	Beartooths	
9	Castle Rock Mountain	12,401	481	Beartooths	
10	Beartooth Mountain	12,351	1471	Beartooths	
11	Bowback Mountain	12,351	711	Beartooths	
12	Glacier Peak	12,351	800	Beartooths	
13	Mount Villard	12,345	545	Beartooths	
14	Mount Hague	12,323	1203	Beartooths	
15	Spirit Mountain	12,283	763	Beartooths	
16	Sundance Mountain	12,262	582	Beartooths	
17	Salo (Darlene) Mountain	12,250	370-410	Beartooths	
18	Cairn Mountain	12,220	840	Beartooths	
19	Mount Rearguard	12,204	1044	Beartooths	
20	Drop Off Mountain	12,115	395-435	Beartooths	
21	Snowbank Mountain	12,084	844	Beartooths	
22	Mystic Mountain	12,080 +	520	Beartooths	
23	Sky Pilot Mountain	12,047	567	Beartooths	
24	Metcalf Mountain	11,977	817	Beartooths	
25	Sylvan Peak	11,935	486	Beartooths	
26	Mount Inabnit	11,928	486	Beartooths	
27	Pk NW of Snowbank Mtn	11,848	448	Beartooths	
28	Mount Wilse	11,831	791	Beartooths	
29	Stillwater Plateau HP	11,817	697	Beartooths	
30	Wolf Mountain	11,816	1120	Beartooths	
31	Twin Peaks	11,793	1233	Beartooths	
32	Summit Mountain	11,704	750	Beartooths	
33	Pk N of Sawtooth Mtn	11,680 +	480	Beartooths	
34	Pk S of Arch Lake	11,576	576	Beartooths	
35	Iceberg Peak	11,552	752	Beartooths	
36	Little Park Mountain	11,505	745	Beartooths	
37	Sawtooth Mountain	11,488	390-430	Beartooths	
38	N Pk of Little Park Mtn	11,480 +	390-430	Beartooths	
39	Mount Hole-in-the-Wall	11,478	478	Beartooths	
40	Pk NW of Big Mtn	11,443	603	Beartooths	
41	Thunder Mountain	11,441	515	Beartooths	
42	Pk E of Summit Mtn	11,440 +	400	Beartooths	
43	Lonesome Mountain	11,400 +	1040	Beartooths	
44	SE Pk of Big Mtn	11,380	460	Beartooths	
45	Pk S of Mt Villard	11,379	539	Beartooths	
46	Big Mountain	11,371	451	Beartooths	
47	Tumble Mountain	11,314	2834	Beartooths	
48	Hilgard Peak	11,297	4044	Madison	
49	Koch Peak	11,293	1173	Madison	
50	Mount Douglas	11,282	1642	Beartooths	
51	Echo Peak	11,250	890	Madison	
52	Mount Fox	11,245	1245	Beartooths	
53	Pk E of Little Park Mtn	11,245	445	Beartooths	
54	Mount Cowen	11,212	2652	Absarokas	
55	Crazy Peak	11,209	5709	Crazies	
56	Imp Peak	11,202	1002	Madison	
57	Two Sisters	11,190	1830	Beartooths	
58	Lone Mountain	11,162	2722	Madison	
59	Tweedy Mountain	11,154	3794	Pioneers	
60	Torrey Mountain	11,147	1107	Pioneers	
61	Chalice Peak	11,146	506	Beartooths	
62	Eighteenmile Peak	11,125	1635	Beaverhead	
63	Pk W of Mt Hague	11,103	1023	Beartooths	
64	Hodges Mountain	11,087	647	Beartooths	
65	Pk N of Summit Mtn	11,086	446	Beartooths	
66	Grass Mountain	11,052	692	Beartooths	
67	Pk W of Koch Pk	11,049	529	Madison	
68	COTTONWOOD BM	11,024	424	Beaverhead	
69	Gallatin Peak	11,015	3197	Madison	
70	Pk NW of Imp Pk	11,000 +	680	Madison	

Montana's Mountain Ranges

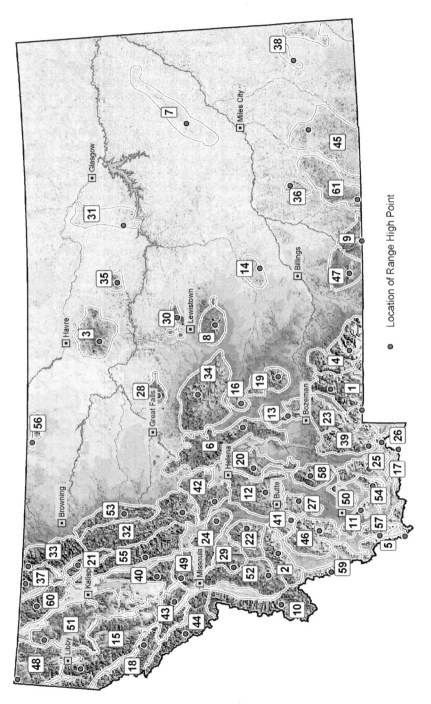

Location of Range High Point ●

Ranges and their Highpoints

#	RANGE	MOUNTAIN	ELEV	PROM	Date Climbed
1	Absaroka Range	**Mount Cowen !	11,212	2652	
2	Anaconda Range	***West Goat Peak	10,793	3953	
3	Bears Paw Mtns	**Bearpaw Baldy	6,916	4226	
4	Beartooth Mtns	**Granite Peak	12,799	4759	
5	Beaverhead Mtns	**Eighteenmile Peak !	11,125	1635	
6	Big Belt Mtns	**Mount Edith	9,507	4107	
7	Big Sheep Mtns	Big Sheep Mtn	3,600	490	
8	Big Snowy Mtns	**Greathouse Peak (1)	8,681	4061	
9	Bighorn Mtns	Stateline Point !	9,257	400	
10	Bitterroot Mtns	**Trapper Peak	10,157	3570	
11	Blacktail Mtns	Blacktail Mtns HP	9,477	2077	
12	Boulder Mtns	**Haystack Mtn	8,819	2379	
13	Bridger Range	**Sacagawea Peak	9,666	3946	
14	Bull Mtns	Dunn Mtn	4,744	904	
15	Cabinet Mtns	**Snowshoe Peak	8,738	5418	
16	Castle Mtns	*Elk Peak	8,566	2766	
17	Centennial Mtns	**Mount Jefferson	10,203	3363	
18	Coeur d'Alene Mtns	Cherry Peak	7,352	2632	
19	Crazy Mtns	**Crazy Peak	11,209	5709	
20	Elkhorn Mtns	**Crow Peak	9,415	3775	
21	Flathead Range	**Great Northern Mtn	8,705	2505	
22	Flint Creek Range	**Mount Powell	10,168	3728	
23	Gallatin Range	**Electric Peak	10,992	3412	
24	Garnet Range	Old Baldy Mtn	7,511	2391	
25	Gravelly Range	Black Butte	10,542	3182	
26	Henrys Lake Mtns	**Pk S of Sheep Mtn	10,606	3666	
27	Highland Mtns	**Table Mtn	10,223	4422	
28	Highwood Mtns	**Highwood Baldy	7,670	3290	
29	John Long Mtns	**Pk E of Quigg Pk	8,468	2548	
30	Judith Mtns	Judith Peak	6,400	1700	
31	Larb Hills	Coal Mine Hill	3,347	992	
32	Lewis & Clark Range	**Red Mtn	9,411	3801	
33	Lewis Range	**Mount Cleveland	10,466	5226	
34	Little Belt Mtns	**Big Baldy Mtn	9,177	3557	
35	Little Rocky Mtns	**Antoine Butte	5,720 +	2670	
36	Little Wolf Mtns	Rosebud County HP	4,807	997	
37	Livingston Range	**Kintla Peak	10,101	4401	
38	Long Pines	**Chalk Buttes HP	4,200 +	720	
39	Madison Range	**Hilgard Peak	11,297	4044	
40	Mission Range	**McDonald Peak	9,820	5640	
41	Mount Fleecer area	Mount Fleecer	9,436	2636	
42	Nevada Mtn area	**Black Mtn	8,330	2530	
43	Nine Mile Creek area	**Ch-paa-qn Peak	7,996	3996	
44	Northern Bitterroots	**QUARTZ BM !	7,770	1890	
45	Otter Creek Mtns	Home Creek Butte	4,407	500	
46	Pioneer Mtns	**Tweedy Mtn	11,154	3794	
47	Pryor Mtns	**Big Pryor Mtn (2)	8,786	4286	
48	Purcell Mtns	**Northwest Peak !	7,705	4424	
49	Rattlesnake Mtns	**McLeod Peak	8,620	3740	
50	Ruby Range	*RUBY BM	9,391	2431	
51	Salish Mtns	**McGuire Mountain	6,991	3071	
52	Sapphire Mtns	Kent Peak	9,000	1750	
53	Sawtooth Range	**Rocky Mtn	9,392	3232	
54	Snowcrest Range	**Sunset Peak	10,581	3741	
55	Swan Range	**Holland Peak	9,356	3996	
56	Sweet Grass Hills	**West Butte	6,983	3633	
57	Tendoy Mtns	Ellis Peak	9,699	1800	
58	Tobacco Root Mtns	**Hollowtop Mtn	10,604	3884	
59	West Big Hole	**Homer Youngs Peak	10,621	3181	
60	Whitefish Range	**Nasukoin Mtn !	8,086	3046	
61	Wolf (Rosebud) Mtns	RED BM	5,450	1200	

! = for Montana portion of the range

(1) = or Old Baldy

(2) = or East Pryor Mtn

Subrange Highpoints and Parent Range

Sub-Range	Parent Range	Highpoint	ELEV	PROM
Adel Mountains	Big Belt Mountains	SIEBEN BM	7,093	1620
Alice Mountains	Lewis & Clark Range	Pk W of Burned Pt	8,135	453
Apgar Mountains	Livingston Range	Apgar Mtns HP	6,651	2771
Bangtail Ridge	Bridger Range	Bangtail Ridge HP	7,982	1830
Bannack Hills	Blacktail Mountains	GRAY BM	7,587	1400
Bull Mountain	Boulder Mountains	BULL BM	8,609	2849
Chalk Buttes	Long Pines	= range HP		
Clark Range (Boundary Mtns)	Livingston Range	Long Knife Peak	9,784	2839
Deer Creek Mountains	Beartooth Mountains	Morning Star Pk HP	9,319	1220
Dickie Hills	Mt Fleecer area	Dickie Peak	9,116	816
Dry Range	Big Belt Mountains	DRY RANGE BM	6,546	1060
East Pioneers	Pioneer Mountains	= range HP		
Ekalaka Hills	Long Pines	Ekalaka Hills HP	4,120 +	530
Flathead Alps	Lewis & Clark Range	Pk W of Junction Mtn	8,360 +	480
Galton Range	Whitefish Range	Poorman Mountain	7,832	1400
Granite Range	Beartooth Mountains	**Mount Wood	12,649 +	2829
Grave Creek Range	Northern Bitterroots	Petty Mountain	7,270	2870
Greenhorn Range	Gravelly Range	Sheep Mountain	9,686	1500
Horseshoe Hills	Big Belt Mountains	GARDEN BM	7,133	1940
John Long Mtns	John Long Mountains	Black Pine Ridge HP	7,937	1197
Lima Peaks	Beaverhead Mountains	**Garfield Mountain	10,961	3281
Limestone Hills	Elkhorn Mountains	Limestone Hills HP	5,976	756
Little Snowy Mountains	Big Snowy Mountains	Bald Butte	5,624	400
London Hills	Elkhorn Mountains	Pk N of Doherty Mtn	6,445	1400
Long Pine Hills	Long Pines	Tri Point Lookout	4,120 +	670
Ninemile Divide	Ninemile Creek area	Stark Mountain	7,352	2232
North Moccasin Mountains	Judith Mountains	North Moccasin	5,603	1500
Quigg Peak area	John Long Mountains	= range HP		
Reservation Divide	Ninemile Creek area	= range HP		
Scratchgravel Hills	Nevada Mtn area	Scratchgravel Hills HP	5,252	730
Smoky Range	Whitefish Range	Standard Peak	7,196	1496
South Moccasin Mountains	Judith Mountains	SOUTH BM	5,798	1740
Spanish Peaks	Madison Range	Gallatin Peak	11,015	3197
Spokane Hills	Elkhorn Mountains	SPOKANE BM	5,517	1190
Thompson Peak area	Cabinet Mountains	**Baldy Mountain	7,464	4064
West Cabinets	Cabinet Mountains	Pk E of Scotchman Pk !	6,933	950
West Pioneers	Pioneer Mountains	Stine Mountain	9,490	1800

! = for Montana portion of Sub-Range

Highest and Biggest Peaks in Montana Counties

(Table on pages 136-137)

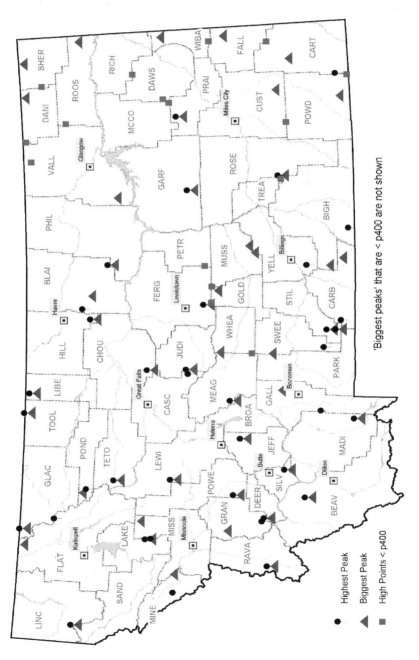

'Biggest peaks' that are < p400 are not shown

Highest Peak

Biggest Peak

High Points < p400

Highest & Biggest Peaks by County

CODE	COUNTY	HIGHEST PEAK	ELEV	PROM	DateClimbed	BIGGEST PEAK	ELEV	PROM	DateClimbed
BEAV	Beaverhead	*Tweedy Mountain	11,154	3794		--same--			
BIGH	Big Horn	Stateline Point	9,257	400		West Pryor Mountain	6,688	1641	
BLAI	Blaine	Pk S of Barber Butte	5,960 +	1400		Black Butte	5,575	1655	
BROA	Broadwater	*Mount Edith	9,507	4107		--same--			
CARB	Carbon	*Castle Mountain	12,612	2652		*Big Pryor Mtn (1)	8,786	4286	
CART	Carter	West Butte	4,450	500		*Chalk Buttes HP	4,200 +	720	
CASC	Cascade	Long Mountain	8,621	781		Mount Cecelia	6,142	2042	
CHOU	Chouteau	*Highwood Baldy	7,670	3290		--same--			
CUST	Custer	<p400				Maxwell Butte	3,726	466	
DANI	Daniels	<p400				Long Butte	2,895	415	
DAWS	Dawson	<p400				<p400			
DEER	Deer Lodge	*West Goat Peak	10,793	3953		--same--			
FALL	Fallon	<p400				SCHWEIGERT BM	3,445	405	
FERG	Fergus	*Greathouse Peak (2)	8,681	4061		--same--			
FLAT	Flathead	*Mount Stimson	10,142	4382		*Kintla Peak	10,101	4401	
GALL	Gallatin	Wilson Peak	10,700	860		*Sacagawea Peak	9,666	3946	
GARF	Garfield	Pk SW of Cohagen	3,660 +	575		--same--			
GLAC	Glacier	*Mount Cleveland	10,466	5226		--same--			
GOLD	Golden Valley	<p400				Sahara Hill	5,481	401	
GRAN	Granite	Warren Peak	10,463	1115		*Pk E of Quigg Pk	8,468	2548	
HILL	Hill	*Bearpaw Baldy	6,916	4226		--same--			
JEFF	Jefferson	*Crow Peak	9,415	3775		--same--			
JUDI	Judith Basin	*Big Baldy Mountain	9,177	3557		--same--			
LAKE	Lake	*McDonald Peak	9,820	5640		--same--			
LEWI	Lewis & Clark	*Red Mountain	9,411	3801		--same--			
LIBE	Liberty	Mount Brown	6,958	3198		--same--			
LINC	Lincoln	*Snowshoe Peak	8,738	5418		--same--			
MADI	Madison	*Hilgard Peak	11,297	4044		--same--			
MCCO	McCone	<p400				<p400			
MEAG	Meagher	*Mount Edith	9,507	4107		--same--			
MINE	Mineral	*QUARTZ BM	7,770	1890		Stark Mountain	7,352	2232	
MISS	Missoula	Lowary Peak (Peak X)	9,369	649		*Holland Peak	9,356	3996	
MUSS	Musselshell	<p400				Three Buttes	4,627	427	
PARK	Park	*Granite Peak	12,799	4759		--same--			
PETR	Petroleum	<p400				<p400			
PHIL	Phillips	*Antoine Butte	5,720 +	2670		--same--			
POND	Pondera	Pk N of Mt Field	8,440 +	960		Half Dome Crag	8,091	2331	
POWD	Powder River	<p400				Bear Skull Mountain	4,300	560	

Highest & Biggest Peaks by County *(con't)*

CODE	COUNTY	HIGHEST PEAK	ELEV	PROM	DateClimbed	BIGGEST PEAK	ELEV	PROM	DateClimbed
POWE	Powell	**Mount Powell	10,168	3728		--same--			
PRAI	Prairie	Big Sheep Mountain	3,600	490		--same--			
RAVA	Ravalli	**Trapper Peak	10,157	3570		--same--			
RICH	Richland	<p400				<p400			
ROOS	Roosevelt	<p400				Snake Butte	2,661	501	
ROSE	Rosebud	Pk W of Colstrip	4,807	997		--same--			
SAND	Sanders	**Snowshoe Peak	8,738	5418		--same--			
SHER	Sheridan	<p400				Pk N of Raymond	2,640	415	
SILV	Silver Bow	**Table Mountain	10,223	4422		--same--			
STIL	Stillwater	**Mount Wood	12,649 +	2809		--same--			
SWEE	Sweet Grass	Mount Douglas	11,282	1642		**Crazy Peak	11,209	5709	
TETO	Teton	**Rocky Mountain	9,392	3232		--same--			
TOOL	Toole	**West Butte	6,983	3633		--same--			
TREA	Treasure	<p400				<p400			
VALL	Valley	<p400				Pk S of Saco	3,179	659	
WHEA	Wheatland	<p400				Pk S of Bluff Mtn	7,588	708	
WIBA	Wibaux	<p400				Blue Mountain	3,077	457	
YELL	Yellowstone	Stratford Hill	4,971	511		Dunn Mountain	4,744	904	

(1) = or East Pryor Mtn   (2) = or Old Baldy

Montana Peaks with more than 2,000 feet of Prominence

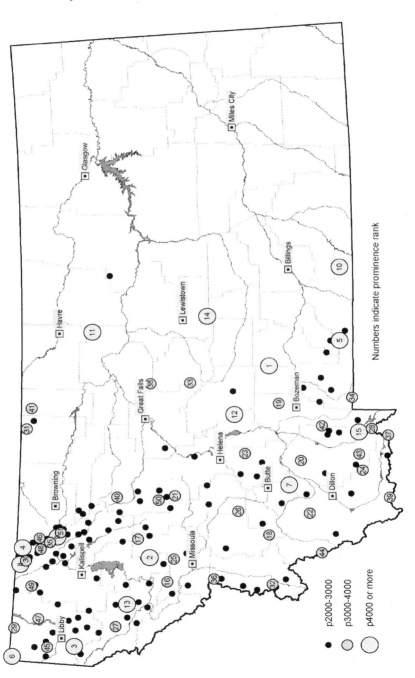

Numbers indicate prominence rank

p2000-3000
p3000-4000
p4000 or more

Montana Peaks with more than 3,000 feet of Prominence

The "prominence" table just lists those peaks with more than 3,000 ft of prominence, rather than all 147 p2000 peaks.

RANK	MOUNTAIN	PROM	ELEV	RANGE	Date Climbed
1	**Crazy Peak	5,709	11,209	Crazies	
2	**McDonald Peak	5,640	9,820	Missions	
3	**Snowshoe Peak	5,418	8,738	Cabinets	
4	**Mount Cleveland	5,226	10,466	Lewis	
5	**Granite Peak	4,759	12,799	Beartooths	
6	**Northwest Peak	4,424	7,705	Purcells	
7	**Table Mountain	4,422	10,223	Highlands	
8	**Kintla Peak	4,401	10,101	Livingston	
9	**Mount Stimson	4,382	10,142	Lewis	
10	**Big Pryor Mountain(1)	4,286	8,786	Pryors	
11	**Bearpaw Baldy	4,226	6,916	Bearpaws	
12	**Mount Edith	4,107	9,507	Belts	
13	**Baldy Mountain	4,064	7,464	Cabinets	
14	**Greathouse Peak(2)	4,061	8,681	Big Snowies	
15	**Hilgard Peak	4,044	11,297	Madison	
16	**Ch-paa-qn (Squaw) Pk	3,996	7,996	Nine Mile	
17	**Holland Peak	3,996	9,356	Swans	
18	**West Goat Peak	3,953	10,793	Pintlers	
19	**Sacagawea Peak	3,946	9,666	Bridgers	
20	**Hollowtop Mountain	3,884	10,604	Tobacco Roots	
21	**Red Mountain	3,801	9,411	Lewis & Clark	
22	**Tweedy Mountain	3,794	11,154	Pioneers	
23	**Crow Peak	3,775	9,415	Elkhorns	
24	**Sunset Peak	3,741	10,581	Snowcrest	
25	**McLeod Peak	3,740	8,620	Rattlesnake	
26	**Mount Powell	3,728	10,168	Flints	
27	Mount Headley	3,716	7,427	Cabinets	
28	**Pk S of Sheep Mtn	3,666	10,606	Henrys Lake	
29	Robinson Mountain	3,639	7,539	Purcells	
30	Rainbow Peak	3,636	9,891	Livingston	
31	**West Butte	3,633	6,983	Sweetgrass	
32	**Trapper Peak	3,570	10,157	Bitterroots	
33	**Big Baldy Mountain	3,557	9,177	Little Belts	
34	**Electric Peak	3,412	10,992	Gallatin	
35	Mount Jackson	3,406	10,052	Lewis	
36	Saint Joseph Peak	3,387	9,587	Bitterroots	
37	**Mount Jefferson	3,363	10,203	Centennials	
38	**Highwood Baldy	3,290	7,670	Highwoods	
39	**Garfield Mountain	3,281	10,961	Beaverhead	
40	**Rocky Mountain	3,232	9,392	Sawtooth	
41	Mount Brown	3,198	6,958	Sweetgrass	
42	Gallatin Peak	3,197	11,015	Madison	
43	Black Butte	3,182	10,542	Gravelly	
44	**Homer Youngs Pk	3,181	10,621	Beaverhead	
45	O'Brien Mountain	3,132	6,772	Purcells	
46	Mount Siyeh	3,106	10,014	Lewis	
47	**McGuire Mountain	3,071	6,991	Salish	
48	Heavens Peak	3,067	8,987	Livingston	
49	**Nasukoin Mountain	3,046	8,086	Whitefish	
50	Scapegoat Mountain	3,042	9,202	Lewis & Clark	
51	Mount Phillips	3,014	9,494	Lewis	

(1) = or East Pryor Mountain

(2) = or Old Baldy

Appendix A: Using UTMs

Another approach to naming peaks is more technical but allows readers to more readily locate the peak. But before reading any further, get out a 7.5 minute topo map. Along the margins of your map, look for two sets of "ticks"—short lines labeled with numbers. One set indicates values of latitude (along the sides) and longitude (along the top and bottom), in degrees, minutes and seconds. The other set indicates UTM coordinates, with values for "northing" along the sides and for "easting" along the top and bottom. These UTM ticks are placed at intervals of 1,000 meters (1 kilometer). The northing values indicate kilometers north of the equator, while the easting values indicate kilometers east from the west boundary of the UTM "zone". The ticks are labeled with the last two digits in larger type: e.g., a northing of 5008 is 5,008 kilometers north of the equator. (The ticks closest to the lower-right and upper-left map corners are labeled in meters, i.e., 5008000m.)

Using these ticks one can estimate (using a ruler) the UTM coordinates for any spot on the map, such as the summit of an unnamed peak. That peak is then identified ('named') using the two numbers in larger type for its easting and northing (and the UTM zone if it's not obvious). For example, the highpoint of the Henrys Lake Mountains is Peak 10,606. It's easting is between (4)69 and (4)70 and its northing is between (49)56 and (49)57. So it could be called Peak UTM 6956. More commonly, peakbaggers interpolate the peak's location to the nearest tenth of a kilometer (100 meters) and identify the peak using three digits for its easting plus three for its northing. In this case it would be Peak UTM 691566.

The Red Mountain bench mark is just left of my poles.

Appendix B: Bench marks and elevation

Bench mark data maintained by the National Geodetic Survey (formerly the Coast & Geodetic Survey) are another source of elevations for those peaks that have a bench mark on their summit. These data are periodically revised in lieu of new or recalculated surveys, and those revisions are often not reflected on the USGS maps.

For example, both the old 15' and new 7.5' topos show the elevation of Granite Peak as 12,799 feet. However, Granite has a bench mark, and if you look up the elevation on its NGS 'Datasheet', it is 12,801 feet (based on the same datum, NGVD 29, as used for USGS maps). Of the peaks discussed in detail in this guide, 28 have bench marks on or near their summits. The USGS and NGS elevations are the same for 13 of these peaks and differ by only one or two feet for another 8. But for the 7 peaks in the table below, the differences are significant.

MOUNTAIN	ELEV-USGS	BENCH MARK	ELEV-NGS
Electric Peak	10,969	ELECTRIC RM 2	10992
Crow Peak	9,415	BOULDER	9432
Sacagawea Peak	9,650	ROSS 2	9666
East Pryor Mountain	8,776	ICE	8787
RUBY BM	9,391	RUBY	9400
Mount Jefferson	10,203	SAWTELLE	10211
Big Pryor Mountain	8,780	SHRIVER	8787

For two of these peaks the differences are readily explained. The elevation shown on the topo map for Electric Peak is actually "10969T". The "T" signifies that this elevation was determined by photogrammetric methods (such as those used to draw contour lines from aerial photos). Why USGS would publish that elevation when a surveyed elevation was available is a mystery. But the same thing happened for Sacagawea Peak, which has an elevation of "9650T" on the topo, but a surveyed elevation of 9670ft according to USGS or 9666ft according to NGS.

Another fact to consider is that bench marks are not always placed at the highest point. For example, the bench mark on Red Mountain in the Scapegoat Wilderness has an elevation of 9411 feet; but it's cemented to a rock that's about 3-4 feet lower than the highest point. Some list-makers try to measure these differences and then include their personally corrected elevations in their lists.

Finally, there are peaks, like East Pryor Mountain, with conflicting elevation data that can't be explained. Each value is supported by properly conducted and calculated surveys and the bench mark is located right on top.

Appendix C: Geodesy, geology, and elevation

Geodesy—our understanding of the shape of the earth.

By elevation we typically mean the height of some point above "mean sea level". So to determine the elevation of a peak in Montana, we need to first figure out where mean sea level is in, or actually under, Montana. Since the earth is not a perfect sphere, that means we must define a mathematical surface that fits the measured values of mean sea level around the world. Then the surveyed heights of peaks or key saddles can be referenced to this mathematical model of mean sea level to compute their elevations.

The 1927 North American Datum (NAD27) and its vertical counterpart, the National Geodetic Vertical Datum of 1929 (NGVD29) (formerly called the "Sea Level Datum of 1929") are based on one such model, the Clarke Ellipsoid of 1866. This ellipsoid was chosen to best fit measurements of sea level around the North American continent. It and its associated datums are still the basis for USGS maps—i.e., for the latitude, longitude and elevation of every feature shown on those maps.

However, the Clarke Ellipsoid is not that good a fit for other parts of the earth (poor old earth is out of shape in more ways than one); so other countries use other models. With the advent of satellites and GPS, geographers started looking for a new model that could be used worldwide. In North America they came up with NAD83 based on the GRS80 ellipsoid, and then the NAVD88—the North American Vertical Datum of 1988. A world-wide variant, WGS84, was also developed in the late 1980s and is now the standard for many applications.   These models and datums do not necessarily produce better or more accurate measures of a peak's elevation—just ones that emanate from a single, world-wide model.

To appreciate how important geodesy and mathematical modeling is, consider the following. Due to its rapid spinning, the Earth's diameter at the equator is 7926 miles, while its diameter pole-to-pole is only 7900 miles. If that 26 mile difference were evenly distributed along a meridian (a line of longitude running between the poles), one can readily calculate that the change is about 11 feet per mile (or 760 feet per degree of latitude). That is, for each mile one moves towards the equator, "mean sea level" bulges 11 feet farther from the center of the Earth. Thus Granite Peak in the Beartooth Mountains (near Montana's southern border) may be 2,333 feet "higher" than Mount Cleveland in Glacier National Park (near Montana's northern border); but it's actually over 5,000 feet farther from the center of the Earth.

Geology—plate tectonics, mountain building (orogeny), and erosion.

Mountains are getting pushed around, and up or down, along with their underlying continental plates; and they are also getting pushed up or down by crunching and fracturing within those plates. For example, the Quake Lake earthquake in 1959 is estimated to have raised the southern Madison Range by 10-15 feet.

Erosion also can change a mountain's elevation. At a landscape level erosion, like mountain "building", occurs in geological time—i.e., very slowly. But for any given spot it often manifests as big, sudden though very infrequent changes, like a landslide or toppling rocks. I'm not aware of any Montana examples, but I do know of a peak in the Wind River Range in Wyoming that lost its top 10 feet or so to natural "mountain top removal". And Mount Saint Helens was the 58th p5000 peak in the "lower 48" before it blew its top!

Conclusion

The take-home lesson is this: don't sweat small variations in numbers. Geographers, listers, and I all report elevations and values of prominence to the foot, but that level of precision barely exists within the surveyor's world of models and reference standards. For the real world—a huge, seething mass of molten matter, coated with a thin crust, spinning and whirling around in space—such precision is illusory.

Appendix D: Some mountain range comparisons

The Tobacco Root Mountains and the Crazy Mountains are two well-defined ranges of about the same size. The Roots have 20 peaks (p400) over 10,000 feet while the Crazies have 21. But in the Roots, 17 of the 20 are named peaks, while in the Crazies only 6 of the 21 have names. Also, there are 16 roads that provide legal access to the Roots but only 5 for the Crazies. I suspect these differences reflect (1) the greater mineralization in the Roots and their rich mining history, and (2) the presence of checkerboard ownership in the Crazies (a legacy of the 1880s railroad land grants), which has restricted access historically and continues to restrict access today.

Glacier National Park and the Absaroka-Beartooth Wilderness are for many folks the premier mountain areas in Montana. Each is about 1 million acres in size (1500+ square miles). The Park has 211 peaks (p400) while the A-B (and adjacent non-wilderness areas) has 207. But the Beartooth Mountains contain all of Montana's 12,000 footers and 61 of Montana's 100 highest peaks. It is far and away the highest range in the state. In contrast, Glacier has eight p3000 peaks (to the A-B's one), 24 p2000 peaks (to the A-B's 6) and 86 p1000 peaks (to the A-B's 44). It is far and away the area with the biggest peaks in the state.

View south from Haystack Mountain, Boulder Mountains.

Bearthooth crest from
Beartooth Butte, Wyoming.

Appendix E:
Montana's 12,000
footers, then & now

This table presents the
elevation and prominence
changes due to finer-scale
mapping and new and
recalculated surveys for
Montana's highest peaks.
The "old" values on the
left are from the 15 minute
topographic maps that were
published before 1955; the
"new" values on the right are
from the 7.5 minute mapping
that was done in the 1980s
and 1990s.

  Besides several changes
in ranking, note that one
peak ("Metcalf Mountain")
is no longer on the list
while another (Snowbank
Mountain) now is. Changes
in the reported elevations of
peaks and their key saddles
have also changed which
peaks meet the p400 (and
p300) prominence standard.

RANK	MOUNTAIN	ELEV	PROM
1	Granite Peak	12,799	
	"NW Pk of Granite"	12,710	230
2	Mount Wood (W Pk)	12,661	2821
3	Castle Mountain	12,612	2612
4	Whitetail Peak	12,548	1348
5	Silver Run Peak (W Pk)	12,542	1502
6	"Castle Rock Spire"	12,529	449
7	Tempest Mountain	12,478	958
8	Mount Peal	12,415	495
9	Castle Rock Mountain	12,408	408
10	Beartooth Mountain	12,377	1497
11	Glacier Peak	12,351	831
12	Bowback Mountain	12,343	663
13	Mount Villard	12,337	577
14	Mount Hague	12,328	1228
15	"Spirit Mountain"	12,240 +	720
16	Sundance Mountain	12,272	512
17	"Cairn Mountain"	12,214	854
18	Mount Rearguard	12,204	1004
	Elk Mountain	12,192	272
	"Salo (Darlene) Mountain"	12,160 +	160
	Pyramid Mountain	12,151	351
19	"Drop Off Mountain"	12,117	437
	"The Spires"	12,160 +	320
	"NE Pk of Castle Rock"	12,080 +	240
20	Mystic Mountain	12,063	543
	"PYRAMID BM"	12,027	177
21	"Metcalf Mountain"	12,019	819
	"Mount Pleasant"	12,006	160
22	"Sky Pilot Mountain"	12,000 +	480
	"Avalanche Mountain"	12,000 +	160
	Snowbank Mountain	11,920 +	640

RANK	MOUNTAIN	ELEV	PROM	Notes
1	Granite Peak	12,799	4759	VABM
	"NW Pk of Granite Pk"	12,745	305-345	
2	Mount Wood (W Pk)	12,649	2809	East Peak higher
3	Castle Mountain	12,612	2652	VABM
4	Whitetail Peak	12,551 T	1271	
5	Silver Run Peak (W Pk)	12,542 T	1505	VABM on East Pk (12,500')
6	Castle Rock Spire	12,540 T	460	
7	Tempest Mountain	12,469	909	
8	Mount Peal	12,409	489	
9	Castle Rock Mountain	12,401 T	481	
10	Beartooth Mountain	12,351 T	1471	
11	Bowback Mountain	12,351	711	
12	Mount Villard	12,345	545	
13	Mount Hague	12,323	1203	
14	Glacier Peak	12,320 +	800	
15	Spirit Mountain	12,283 T	763	
16	Sundance Mountain	12,262 T	582	
	Elk Mountain	12,256	256-296	
17	"Salo (Darlene) Mountain"	12,250 T	370-410	SW of Castle Rock Mtn
18	Mount Rearguard	12,204	1044	VABM
19	Cairn Mountain	12,200 +	840	Elev = 12,220 in GNIS
	Pyramid Mountain	12,119	319-359	
20	"Drop Off Mountain"	12,115 T	395-435	NW of Spirit Mtn
	"NE Pk of Castle Rock"	12,090 T	290-330	
21	Snowbank Mountain	12,084 T	844	
22	Mystic Mountain	12,080 +	520	
23	Sky Pilot Mountain	12,047 T	567	
	PYRAMID BM	12,022	182-222	
	"Mount Pleasant"	12,009 T	169-209	SE of Mount Peal
	The Spires	12,000 +	280-360	
	"Avalanche Mountain"	12,000 +	160-240	SW of Beartooth Mtn
	"Metcalf Mountain"	11,977 T	817	SSE of Spirit Mtn

Terminology used in this guide

This guide uses some terms that may be new to you or used in new ways.

3rd class (class 3): a level of scrambling where the hands are used to climb, but you are comfortable climbing without a rope.

Belt formation: a thick band of very old rock, mostly shale, that dominates NW Montana. It is often red, green or gray; it often has ripple marks and mud cracks; and it often forms lots of short cliffs and ledges.

bench mark: a survey monument, typically a small metal disc cemented to solid rock.

blaze: a gouge in the bark of a tree, usually made with an axe, used to mark the trail. FS blazes are a distinctive dot-over-dash shape.

cairn: a pile or stack of rocks used to mark a trail.

deadfall: dead trees, or fire-killed trees, that have fallen over.

dog-hair: small, very closely-spaced trees.

dogleg: a pair of sharp turns in opposite directions that offset a route to the left or right.

drainage: the low ground that carries runoff from rain or melting snow. Small-scale valleys, located between ridges or spurs. A gully is a very small drainage; a couloir is a very small, steep and rocky drainage.

exposure, exposed: a place that makes you feel afraid of falling

gnarly: a landscape that is difficult to bushwhack in or through, due to deadfall or repro or thick trees or brush or big boulders or loose rocks or any combination of the above.

inholding: a parcel of private land entirely surrounded by public land or located within the boundary of a designated site, like a state or national park.

key saddle: a peak's key saddle is the highest saddle between that peak and any higher terrain.

krumholz: a German word for the stunted, twisted and often dense tree growth found at timberline.

peak: a high point of ground. For this guide, "peak" denotes a highpoint with at least 400 feet of prominence, and a "blip" is a really minor point.

repro (short for reproduction): dense clusters or a carpet of baby trees that come in after a fire. Repro often grows up to become dog-hair.

ridge: a line of high ground that separates drainages (a.k.a. "drainage divide"). A spur (spur ridge) is a small ridge that breaks up the face of a major ridge. A reef is a ridge formed by up-thrust rock layers – it is cliffy on one side and smooth-sloped on the other.

scrambling: walking means moving without any use of your hands; climbing means the constant use of hands is necessary, plus the use of a rope for safety. Scrambling is everything in between.

scree: broken up rock, typically lying on a slope. Scree is rock pieces bigger than sand but small enough to walk on like sand. Talus is pieces large enough to stand on. Rubble (sometimes 'cobble') is the awkward size in between scree and talus. Blocks are pieces so big you need to use your hands to maneuver over and around them.

sidehill: a route that crosses a slope (as opposed to going straight up or down the slope, or to walking on level ground). "Traverse" means to travel across a slope; "contour" means to traverse without gaining or losing elevation.

use (user) trail: a trail created by the repeated passage of people (or stock or vehicles) over the same route.

veg: as used in this guide = the mix of forbs, grasses and mat-like plants typically found above timberline. Veg often mixes with talus, rubble, sometimes even scree, in varying proportions.

Abbreviations

Directions: **N,S,E,W** etc.
ATV = all-terrain vehicle
BLM = Bureau of Land Management
BM = bench mark
    (VABM = vertical angle bench mark)
BP = biggest peak (most prominent peak)
CDT = Continental Divide Trail
CSKT = Confederated Salish & Kootenai Tribes
ELEV = elevation (in feet)
FS = US Forest Service
GNIS = Geographic Names Information
        System
GPS = global positioning system
HP = highpoint
ks = key saddle

MFWP = Montana Fish, Wildlife & Parks
MP (+ a number) = highway mile post
NF = National Forest
NGS = National Geodetic Survey
NP = National Park
NPS = National Park Service
NRT = National Recreation Trail
ORV = off-road-vehicle (motorcycle, ATV)
Pk = peak
PROM = prominence (in feet)
  p400 = a 400 ft prominence standard
  p 400' = a specific prominence of 400 ft
RT = round trip
USGS = US Geological Survey
TH = trailhead

One peakbagger's best friend atop Trapper Peak. (Christopher Cauble photo)

Index

The author on the Nose of the Sleeping Giant, north of Helena. (B.Bucher photo)

Note: **Bold type** indicates a featured peak.

View from upper Layout Creek, East Pryor Mountain.

NOTES

NOTES

View south from Hilgard Peak, Madison Range.

MORE GREAT BOOKS FOR
EXPLORING MONTANA

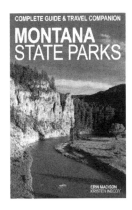

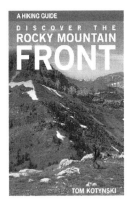

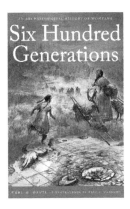

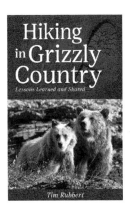

Look for these and other Montana books at your local bookstore or at riverbendpublishing.com